Inside Heaven's Gates

Inside Heaven's Gates

E. M. BOUNDS

Whitaker House

INSIDE HEAVEN'S GATES

ISBN: 0-88368-569-8
Printed in the United States of America
Copyright © 1985 by Whitaker House

Whitaker House
30 Hunt Valley Circle
New Kensington, PA 15068

Library of Congress Cataloging-in-Publication Data

Bounds, Edward M. (Edward McKendree), 1835–1913.
    Inside heaven's gates / by E. M. Bounds.
        p.   cm.
    ISBN 0-88368-569-8 (pbk.)
    1. Heaven—Christianity. 2. Future life—Christianity. I. Title.
BT846.2.B68   1999
236'.24—dc21   99-24258

2 3 4 5 6 7 8 9 10 11 12 13 / 07 06 05 04 03 02 01 00 99

CONTENTS

INTRODUCTION

While pastoring in Atlanta, I was informed that there was an apostolic man of prayer in Georgia that would aid the church in spiritual things. I sent a letter asking Mr. Bounds to come to our convention for ten days' preaching. We expected to see a man of imposing physique, but when he came we discovered that he was only about five and a half feet tall. In him we met one of the greatest saints that has appeared on the spiritual horizon in the last hundred years.

He spoke the first afternoon on prayer. No one seemed to be particularly impressed. The next morning at 4 a.m. we were amazed to hear him engaged in the most wonderful prayer we had ever listened to—a prayer that seemed to take in both heaven and earth. His sermons were all about *prayer* and *heaven*.

Not one morning during his stay did he fail to pray. He cared nothing about the protests of the other occupants of his room at being àwakened at an unheard-of hour. No man could have made more melting appeals for lost souls and backslidden ministers than did Mr. Bounds. Tears ran down his face as he pleaded for us all in that room. I know of no other man on earth today who, if he had followed the same experiment at the same place and in the same room, would have gone away undefeated. But Mr. Bounds was powerful, commanding, and victorious when he knew his cause was just.

After that convention we took him in to our hearts and never let him go. God sent him in answer to prayer to settle and establish me in the things of God that are foremost and supreme— prayer, preaching, and the study of the Bible.

We were constantly with him, in prayer and preaching, for eight precious years. Not a foolish word did we ever hear him utter. He was one of the most intense eagles of God that ever penetrated the spiritual sky.

Homer W. Hodge

Chapter 1

HEAVEN IS A PLACE

"If you saw a man shut up in a small room, idolizing a set of lamps and rejoicing in their light, and you wanted to make him truly happy, you would begin by blowing out all his lamps and throwing open the shutters to let in the light of heaven"—Samuel Rutherford.

Death does not and cannot end all. Man must exist for all eternity, and the future may be one of unutterable bliss. Heaven does not float around. It is not made of air. It is real—a country, a climate, and a home where sacred affections draw us. Divine assurance settles and fixes the fact.

Heaven may be a reality or simply a state of being. The Bible teaches it is a *place* with a definite location in contrast to an unsettled and temporary pilgrim state.

The strong argument for heaven as a place centers in and clusters about Jesus. The man Jesus, bearing the body He wore on earth, has a place assigned to Him—a high place.

"Wherefore God also hath highly exalted him, and given him a name which is above every name: That at the name of Jesus every knee should bow, of things in heaven, and things in earth, and things under the earth; And that every tongue should confess that Jesus Christ is Lord, to the glory of God the Father" (Philippians 2:9-11).

"Which he wrought in Christ, when he raised him from the dead, and set him at his own right hand in the heavenly places, Far above all principality, and power, and might, and dominion, and every name that is named, not only in this world, but also in that which is to come: And hath put all things under his feet, and gave him to be the head over all things to the church, Which is his body, the fulness of him that filleth all in all" (Ephesians 1:20-23).

This indicates a place of high honor, the best and most royal in the heavenly world.

"God who at sundry times and in divers manners spake in time past unto the fathers by the prophets, Hath in these last days spoken unto us by his Son, whom he hath appointed heir to all things, by whom also he made the worlds; Who being the brightness of his glory, and the express image of his person, and upholding all things by the word of his power, when he had by himself purged our sins, sat down on the right hand of the Majesty on high" (Hebrews 1:1-3).

These verses address His place in God's many-mansioned country. "Who is gone into heaven, and is on the right hand of God; angels and authorities and powers being made subject unto him" (1 Peter 3:22).

These are figures of Christ's exaltation and location. They are figures of a place. Jesus wants us with Him to see and share His glory. He dwells in a place that honors and glorifies His person and presence. His business is to prepare a place for us.

"Father, I will that they also, whom thou hast given me, be with me where I am; that they may behold my glory, which thou hast given me" (John 17:24).

The Journey's End

Heaven in the Bible is represented as a place in contrast with earth. The earth is a place, but it is unstable, insecure, and fleeting. Heaven is stable, secure, and eternal.

"For here have we no continuing city, but we seek one to come" (Hebrews 13:14).

The contrast between earth and heaven is remarkable! Earth is a pilgrim's stay, a pilgrim's journey, and a pilgrim's tent. Heaven is a city, permanent, God-planned, and God-built, whose foundations are as stable as God's throne.

"By faith Abraham, when he was called to go out into a place which he should after receive for an inheritance, obeyed; and he went out not knowing whither he went. By faith, he sojourned in the land of promise, as in a strange country, dwelling in tabernacles with Issac and Jacob, the heirs with him of the same promise: For he looked for a city which hath foundations, whose builder and maker is God" (Hebrews 11:8-9).

The Bible reveals heaven as a place. It is measured off with appointed boundaries like an actual walled city. Heaven is inside and hell is outside.

"For without are dogs, and sorcerers, and whoremongers, and murderers, and idolaters, and whosoever loveth and maketh a lie" (Revelation 22:15).

Heaven is a *place*. "I go," said Jesus, "to prepare a *place* for you" (John 14:2). That means locality, something settled. Heaven has its boundaries on God's map. In God's house, Jesus declares, are many mansions. The New Version has in the margin, "abiding places." In God's many homes, one home was to be theirs, a place prepared for them. This was the comfort to the disciples, saddened as they were. "Going to prepare a place for them" is the purpose and fact in Christ's departure. Nothing can be simpler, more explicit, or more honest than this revelation to them of Christ's purpose and plans.

It is as though He had said, "Earth is a place where we have been abiding. We can abide together no longer here, but God has many other places. I go to select one of these places for you. When it is ready I will come and take you there, and we will be together in place and in spirit, 'that where I am, there ye may be also' " (John 14:3).

Our Préparation And Inheritance

Jesus said, "prepare a place." The term means to make the necessary preparations and get everything ready. It is a figure drawn from the eastern custom of sending persons before kings to level the roads and make them passable. Jesus is our pioneer, gone to prepare heaven for us. Its model was Canaan, a prepared place. Israel did not have to pioneer the way. Homes and cities were already built for them. They had nothing to do except enter in, possess, and enjoy. But Canaan was a feeble type, so its preparation was only a faint shadow of the preparation that will be made for us in heaven, a God-built city.

As Jesus Christ drew near to the end, important things engaged His attention. He must commit to His disciples the interests of His Kingdom. Heaven was all-important. Heaven was to be kept in eye and heart all the time. Their deep spiritual life, their personal holiness, and their conscious abiding in Christ were all important. Christ spoke of the necessity of Christ-life and Christ-likeness in His last sacred words.

What could be clearer, more hope-giving, or more conclusive than the words of Christ on the verge of His going away? His disciples were sorrowfully impressed, deeply touched, and depressed by the thought of His leaving. He challenged their faith in Himself and linked Himself as the object of their faith in God.

Peter viewed heaven as a place, an inheritance to be sought for, and a possession awaiting us. He is just as enraptured by the glorious vision as Paul.

"Blessed be the God and Father of our Lord Jesus Christ, which according to his abundant mercy hath begotten us again unto a lively hope by the resurrection of Jesus Christ from the dead, To an inheritance incorruptible, and undefiled, and that fadeth not away, reserved in heaven for you, Who are kept by the power of God through faith unto salvation ready to be revealed in the last time" (1 Peter 1:3-5).

Heaven is not merely a name. It is a tangible state with local inhabitants.

John had a picture of heaven. The picture is for charm, comfort, and strength.

"After this I beheld, and, lo, a great multitude, which no man could number, of all nations, and kindreds, and people, and tongues, stood before the throne, and before the Lamb, clothed with white robes, and palms in their hands; And cried with a loud voice, saying, Salvation to our God which sitteth upon the throne, and unto the Lamb. And all the angels stood round about the throne, and about the elders and the four beasts, and fell before the throne on their faces, and worshipped God, Saying, Amen: Blessing, and glory, and wisdom, and thanksgiving, and honor, and power, and might, be unto our God for ever and ever. Amen. And one of the elders answered, saying unto me, What are these which are arrayed in white robes?

and whence came they? And I said unto him, Sir, thou knowest. And he said to me, These are they which came out of great tribulation, and have washed their robes, and made them white in the blood of the Lamb. Therefore are they before the throne of God, and serve him day and night in his temple: and he that sitteth on the throne shall dwell among them. They shall hunger no more, neither thirst any more; neither shall the sun light upon them, nor any heat. For the Lamb which is in the midst of the throne shall feed them, and shall lead them unto living fountains of waters: and God shall wipe away all tears from their eyes" (Revelation 7:9-17).

"To day shalt thou be with me in Paradise" (Luke 23:43) was the answer of Jesus to the prayer of the thief on the cross. "Through the gates into the city" (Revelation 22:14) represents a place. "Absent from the body, and to be present with the Lord" (2 Corinthians 5:8) indicates locality. Elijah and Enoch are in their bodies. (See 2 Kings 2:11; Genesis 5:24.)

The future of the saints will not be vague and transitory but defined, limited, and real as soul and body will be real. The glorified will not be pilgrims, transient visitors, or tenants at will but settled and permanent, established by title through eternity. There will be no tenants in heaven but all will be property and home-owners. Heaven's patent is issued to guarantee right and title. In fact, it is ours before we get there. It is reserved and guarded for us; our names of ownership are engraven and jeweled on our heavenly home.

Away from earth's forlorn decay
Jerusalem doth shine;
Transfigured hands applaud its King,
Majestic and Refined.

No eye can see nor ear doth hear,
The melodies that play
Upon the strings of Light and Love,
In Zion's timeless Day!

Chapter 2

A HOUSE NOT MADE WITH HANDS

"For we know that if our earthly house of this tabernacle were dissolved we have a building of God, an house not made with hands eternal in the heavens"—2 Corinthians 5:1.

In this Scripture the apostle contrasts a tent's frail and temporary nature and the permanency of heaven. All earthly houses, however beautiful, costly, and enduring they may be, are made with earthly hands and are subject to decay. The marks of their ruin are on them, laid in their very foundations. The houses of heaven are God-built and are as enduring and incorruptible as their builder.

We will have bodies after the resurrection, transfigured after the model of Christ's glorious body. The transfiguration will refine and spiritualize the substance of our bodies, but we will require houses then to live in as we do now. What houses they will be! Fitted essentially for every use, employment, and enjoyment of the heavenly citizens, they will reflect honor on and bring glory to God by their untold beauty and magnificence.

Whatever Paul may mean, whether it is used to signify the glorious body that will be the residence of our spirits, or whether he refers to some structure outside of ourselves, it is all the same God-built mansion for body and spirit immortalized.

Paul again asserts the security and confidence of heaven: "We are confident, I say, and willing rather to be absent from the body, and to be present with the Lord" (2 Corinthians 5:3).

Home is always a place—the heart's place—to which longings draw and around which sweet memories cluster.

Paul was caught up into paradise, into the third heaven. These passages and others have in them, in intention and spirit, a place. Lazarus was carried by the angels to Abraham's bosom.

In the Bible it is taken for granted that heaven is stable, enduring, and attractive, in contrast with the transitory conditions of earth. If the description in the Revelation of John is in any way a description of the material aspect of heaven, the place is one of matchless and exquisite beauty, "incorruptible, and undefiled, and that fadeth not away" (1 Peter 1:4).

Stephen, the first martyr, was a man full of faith and the Holy Spirit. In the presence of a cruel, murderous death and an infuriated mob, he had the sight and peace of heaven.

"But he, being full of the Holy Ghost, looked up steadfastly into heaven, and saw the glory of God, and Jesus standing on the right hand of God, And said, Behold, I see the heavens opened, and the Son of man standing on the right hand of God. Then they cried out with a loud voice, and stopped their ears, and ran upon him with one accord, And cast him out of the city, and stoned him: and the witnesses laid down their clothes at a young man's feet whose name was Saul. And they stoned Stephen, calling upon God, and saying, Lord Jesus, receive my spirit. And he kneeled down, and cried with a loud voice, Lord, lay not this sin to their charge. And when he had said this, he fell asleep" (Acts 7:55-60).

Revealing The Kingdom

Jesus declared, "I came down from heaven" (John 6:38). We will learn much from Him of heaven. From heaven He came, and for heaven He suffered. In heaven He lived and to heaven He returned. Born in heaven, living in heaven, breathing the air of heaven, speaking the language of heaven, and longing for heaven, it would be strange if we did not hear much of heaven from His lips.

In familiar language He impresses us with the fact that heaven is a place. His memorable conversation with Nicodemus is a contrast between earth and heaven.

"If I have told you earthly things, and ye believe

not, how shall he believe, if I tell you of heavenly things? And no man hath ascended up to heaven, but he that came down from heaven, even the Son of man which is in heaven" (John 3:12-13).

We are assured that we will hear much from Jesus about heaven. He begins His beatitudes, "Blessed are the poor in spirit; for theirs is the kingdom of heaven" (Matthew 5:3).

The Sermon on the Mount begins with heaven. He teaches us to let our light shine that we may glorify our Father in heaven; that unless our righteousness exceed the righteousness of the scribes and Pharisees, we will not enter into the Kingdom. He begins His divine mission with heaven accepted and recognized as a matter of importance, in full force and to the front. His early preaching was saturated with the principles of heaven. "Repent," He said, "for the kingdom of heaven is at hand" (Matthew 4:17).

The foundation stone of spiritual character is cemented and infused with the same theme. The first utterance of His sermon is a beatitude of the Kingdom of heaven. The diamond of character is "Blessed are the pure in heart: for they shall see God" (Matthew 5:8). Seeing, knowing, and loving God includes and finds its full realization in heaven. To see Him in everything—in every tear that dims the eye or breaks the heart—is heaven begun on earth. To see God is the highest heaven. "For now we see through a glass, darkly; but then face to face: now I know in part; but then shall I

20

know even as also I am known" (1 Corinthians 13:12).

He brings us into the presence of His children and their character, and we see the child's inheritance: "if children, then heirs" (Romans 8:17). "Blessed are the peacemakers: for they shall be called the children of God" (Matthew 5:9).

The next beatitude reads, "Blessed are they which are persecuted for righteousness' sake: for theirs is the kingdom of heaven." This leads the way to the last: "Blessed are ye, when men shall revile you, and persecute you, and shall say all manner of evil against you falsely, for my sake. Rejoice, and be exceeding glad: for great is your reward in heaven: for so persecuted they the prophets which were before you" (Mark 5:10-12).

Discipleship—Conduct And Character

Jesus in His first call to discipleship stimulates and connects that call with all the comfort and hope of heaven. Heaven is at the foundation of the system of Jesus, its first thought, brightest hope, and strongest faith. Their Father, He tells them, is in heaven, and they must reflect glory on their Father. The righteousness of His followers must exceed the righteousness of the scribes and the Pharisees or else the glories of heaven will never be theirs. Commonplace piety will *not* bring heaven.

Jesus taught that heaven is God's throne and the

earth is His footstool. As the throne excels in honor, character, and material, and uses the earthly footstool, so does heaven excel earth. Jesus will not let it get out of their minds that their Father is in heaven, a place defined and located, and that they are His children. They must be like Him to share His character, imitate His conduct, and share His heaven. Heaven is His home. The Father's character must be the children's character, the Father's conduct must be the children's conduct, the Father's place must be the children's place, and the Father's home must be the children's home.

"Ye have heard that it hath been said, Thou shalt love thy neighbour, and hate thine enemy. But I say unto you, Love your enemies, bless them that curse you, do good to them that hate you, and pray for them which despitefully use you, and persecute you; That ye may be the children of your Father which is in heaven: for he maketh his sun to rise on the evil and the good, and sendeth rain on the just and on the unjust. For if ye love them which love you, what reward have ye? do not even the publicans the same? And if ye salute your brethren only, what do ye more than others? do not even the publicans so? Be ye therefore perfect, even as your Father which is in heaven is perfect" (Matthew 5:43-48).

Charity, prayer, and fasting take their character and their obligation from *"Our Father who art in heaven"* (Matthew 6:9). Heaven is His dwelling place and receives its glory from the Father. The Father's name and the Father's dwelling place are to be reverenced. Earth ought to look to heaven's harmony, beauty, and ecstasy, all due to obedience to God's will, and learn how to rival heaven. But instead, earth is devoted to its own fashions and is ready to forget the higher and holier place that should be its type.

Jesus keeps the being, the order, and the beauty of heaven ever before us and hangs them all around the Father's house, decorating His abode, saying, "Be like God. He is your Father. Children, be like your Father. Heaven is His home. Make your home like His."

Where Is Your Treasure?

Jesus said the earth is not safe. Thieves are here, and treasures are lost here. Moths are here. The finest silks and costliest robes are eaten. Our richest jewels and finest gold corrode and rust. Heaven is a place of absolute safety. No robberies ever occur on its plains or in its cities. Moths are not known there. Its spotless robes have never been defiled. Its precious stones and metals don't know the touch of rust. All is pure, polished, glittering, and forever secure. The command for safety and obedience is emphatic and absolute!

"Lay not up for yourselves treasures upon earth, where moth and rust doth corrupt, and where thieves break through and steal: But lay up for yourselves treasures in heaven, where neither moth nor rust doth corrupt, and where thieves do not break through nor steal: For where your treasure is, there will your heart be also. The light of the body is the eye: if therefore thine eye be single, thy whole body shall be full of light. But if thine eye be evil, thy whole body shall be full of darkness. If therefore the light that is in thee be darkness, how great is that darkness!" (Matthew 6:19-23).

The divine Teacher emphasizes heaven! He wants our hearts to be there. The heart is the soul and being of the man. Safety is in heaven. No tears are there to flood your heart, no sorrows there to break it, and no losses there to grieve and embitter. Put your heart in heaven that it may be sweet, whole, and joyful. Put your treasures in heaven and all will be light. Don't divide yourself between heaven and earth.

"No man can serve two masters: for either he will hate the one and love the other; or else he will hold to the one and despise the other. Ye cannot serve God and mammon" (Luke 16:13).

Anxiety about food and clothing have mastered many souls, breeded fears, and uprooted faith. Jesus Christ shows that the cause of these anxieties results from lack of faith in our Father in heaven. As their only infallible cure, He puts on an absorbing pursuit of heaven: "Seek ye first the kingdom of God, and his righteousness; and all these things shall be added unto you" (Matthew 6:33).

Jesus wants to quiet our anxieties by stressing

that our "Heavenly Father knoweth that ye have need of all these things" (Matthew 6:32). He links us with our Father and His ability and concern for us. With heaven as His abode and ours, Jesus would calm our hearts and set them on heaven and its pursuits. This is impossible when earthly needs confuse us. To Jesus, heaven is the real place; it is the Father's home.

> *Let others seek a home below,*
> *Which flames devour, or waves o'erflow,*
> *Be mine a happier lot, to own*
> *A heavenly mansion near the throne.*

> *Then fail this earth, let stars decline,*
> *And sun and moon refuse to shine,*
> *All nature sink and cease to be,*
> *That heavenly mansion stands for me*
> *—William Hunter.*

Chapter 3

HEAVEN IS A CITY

"If contentment were here, heaven would not be heaven. I wonder why a child of God would ever have a sad heart, considering what his Lord is preparing for him."—Samuel Rutherford.

Heavenly and divine, the city is shaped and built by God. The heavenly life will come from God directly and will be heavenly, not earthly. Many happenings and events shape our earthly lives. But in a direct and evident way, our heavenly lives will be from God; and the conditions of heaven will shape them. Former things will not be forgotten but crowded out, overwhelmed by the magnificent grandeur of the present. Earth will be too little. Its most sacred relationships and most pleasing things will be all too poor to come into mind in heaven.

"And I John saw the holy city, new Jerusalem, coming down from God out of heaven, prepared as a bride adorned for her husband. And I heard a great voice out of heaven saying, Behold, the tabernacle of God is with men, and he will dwell with them, and they shall be his people, and God himself shall be with them, and be their God. And God shall wipe away all tears from their eyes; and there shall be no more death, neither sorrow, nor crying, neither shall there be any more pain: for the former things are passed away. And he that sat upon the throne said, Behold, I make all things new'' (Revelation 21:2-5).

A transfigured mind and memory, a purified thought and love, and a transfigured body shining like a sun in noonday splendor will be the saint's eternal inheritance. God's power and glory make all things new—a bride adorned for her husband, the marriage hour, and the bridal array—all are emblems of the marriage of heaven and earth on their festal day. Perfect beauty, perfect taste, and perfect joy will be heaven's honeymoon.

All Things Become New

The tabernacle refers to the place where God dwelled and manifested Himself to Moses. God will be immediately present with men in the heavenly world in ways that He is not with them in this life. They will draw their life and blessing directly from Him. "And I saw no temple therein: for the Lord God Almighty and the Lamb are the temple of it. And the city had no need of the sun, neither of the moon, to shine in it; for the glory of God did lighten it, and the Lamb is the light thereof'' (Revelation 21:22-23).

Again it is said: "And they need no candle, neither light of the sun; for the Lord God giveth them light" (Revelation 22:5). In this life we cannot understand this. Secondary causes are the agencies through which God ministers to us in this world. In heaven these agencies will not intervene and hide God, but we will see Him face to face. There will be no temple, no temple service, and no brilliant sun. The glory of God, brighter than the light of a thousand suns, will be our light. The mild, sweet rays from the Lamb will cast their radiance over all the land, scattering darkness, gloom, and sorrow. "For there shall be no night there" (Revelation 21:25).

In heaven no tears will be shed, for God will wipe all tears from our eyes. "There shall be no death, neither sorrow nor crying nor pain." How difficult to imagine such a changed world! Tears are the sad heritage of this life. Sorrow and pain flow from a thousand sources and deepen, widen, and darken earth's sorrow. Our sweetest relationships give birth to our greatest sorrows. Our distresses often flow from our joys. Death reigns.

All this will be changed, and everything that gives pain and sorrow will be barred from heaven forever. How bright the eyes undimmed by a tear! How strong and free our souls and bodies will be, utter and eternal strangers to pain! How bright and joyous our hearts, with never a cloud or a sorrow. How full of the richest life, untouched by decay and unshadowed by death, heaven will be!

All things are to be made new. There will be no marks of age, no common things, and no freshened or repainted old things. All things will be absolutely new. A new world, a new life, a new career, a new history, a new environment, a new employment, and a new destiny—*all* things will be new. World dreams, pictures, poetry, fiction, and music have all failed to give the idea of that new world and its marvelous life. To live there is rapture. Its climax is, "He that overcometh shall inherit all things; and I will be his God, and he shall be my son" (Revelation 21:7). It is the wonder and spectacle of angels.

Type and shadow, precept and promise, both in the Old and New Testaments, are tokens and seals of the saints' inheritance after death. No truth is more necessary to man and more in accordance with God's character, none more necessary to His glory, than the doctrine of heaven. An eternal heaven of purity and bliss through endless years is a doctrine that enables man and honors God. The existence of heaven and its matchless perfection is a truth based upon the advent, person, and work of Jesus Christ. Christ is the way to heaven.

The Nature Of Heaven

Heaven lies beyond this life. It is located in another world. The boundary line, death, must be crossed before its gates can be entered and its happy land possessed and enjoyed.

Among the many illustrations that convey the

nature of heaven to us, the illustration of a city is the most striking. It seems to clearly and fully communicate the idea and characteristic of that unseen land. A city teems with life in its richest and most strenuous form. It has never felt the chill of death. It is unlimited by conditions or time and unrestrained by any of the environments of this earthly life. Graves have never been dug there, cemeteries are unknown, and tombstones and coffins are alien. Heaven is a city of life. It is majestic and glorious. Heaven knows no tears and has never felt a sorrow. It is filled with eternal, brilliant, and vibrant life.

A city is a picture of closest union. Life there is forced into closest proximity. Unity, compactness, and nearness are the essentials of city life.

Earth is broken into discord, but heaven is a place of unity. There are no distances in heaven. It is called the "beloved city" (Revelation 20:9). Affections center in heaven, and longings go there in strong, restless current. The beloved of earth and the beloved of heaven have turned their feet to heaven and placed their heart's dearest love there. Angels hold it in their tenderest love. Friends are there. In that city they have found their home. Centuries have come and gone since the tired feet of earth's saintly pilgrims found sweet rest in heaven. None ever go out of that city. Love holds them in.

"The city of my God," says Christ, "the city of the living God. God hath prepared for them a city, a city that hath foundations, whose maker and builder is God" (Revelation 3:12; Hebrews 11:10-16; 12:22). God has everything to do with that city. He drew its plans and laid its deep foundations. God built it, fitted it, and finished it. All life is there, direct from God. In its fullness, vigor, and brightness, God is its life.

God is its architect and contractor; no archangel's matchless taste and incomparable genius were used in drafting the plan of this glorious city. God drew the plan. The stores of God's own wisdom, divine skill, and faultless taste brought into perfection the design of heaven. God was its builder. Only he could carry out the original. The God who laid the deep foundations of the world and brought into being and order its mighty movements stoops to enter again into the work of creation and builds a home for His children.

No night rests on this heavenly city. It is emphatically called, "the city of the living God." God is more immediately, more personally, and more gloriously there than elsewhere. Life is there with God as its immediate source and supply. It contains life in its richest fullness, sweet, gracious, and attractive. Free from all that could affect the perfection of its joy or restrain its endless advance, heaven is a glorious city—God-built with glorious inhabitants. It would be a little heaven to see the city and get a sight of its princely citizens.

The New Jerusalem

It is a city protected by jeweled walls. A city was a treasure deposit, and its walls kept it safe. Heaven is called the New Jerusalem not only to distinguish it from the historical Jerusalem but also to designate its freshness. Never is it to know decay or dullness. It is called the heavenly Jerusalem to emphasize its glories.

The earthly Jerusalem was the center of the hopes of the Jewish people, and their hearts were there as well. There was no song but only sadness and exile when they were away from it. Their hearts always trembled to that pole, and their prayers were made with windows open to Jerusalem. All this symbolizes what the heavenly Jerusalem should be to us. "If I forget thee, O Jerusalem, let my right hand forget her cunning. If I do not remember thee, let my tongue cleave to the roof of my mouth; if I prefer not Jerusalem above my chief joy" (Psalm 137:5-6). Heaven ought to be far more to us than Jerusalem was to the Jew. In this "we groan, earnestly desiring to be clothed upon with our house which is from heaven" (2 Corinthians 5:2).

These Bible symbols are designed to draw, stir, and instruct us in the nature of heaven as far as language can convey eternal and heavenly things. Heaven is called a city by the Bible. This is a familiar Bible symbol of heaven—the great foundational city of the living God. It is not by accident that this term is a common and favorite one. It suggests heaven's manifold nature.

Out of respect for Jewish sanctities, and as a memorial, it was called "The New Jerusalem." The Jew will find full compensation for the loss of his earthly Jerusalem in this new city, which will endure eternally.

The term "city" is a familiar type of heavenly land and heavenly life. A city is the center of power and life, and heaven is a great city. All the principles and facts that the term "city" bring to mind find their full expression there. A jeweled and a golden city express the unsurpassed loveliness and preciousness of that country and its life. Jewels are in the foundations of its walls, and its pavements are made of gold. The most costly materials of earth are used for the lowest and most common uses of heaven. We have no figures or values to represent the exceeding richness of its higher things. It is God's capital, overflowing with all the glory of His presence.

Heaven is called a city in reference to the original meaning of the word city: "fullness, throng." Heaven will be full. An innumerable company which no man can number will gather within its walls. (See Hebrews 12:22 and Revelation 7:9.) Its thoroughfares will be crowded, and its golden pavements pressed by throngs of enraptured feet.

The road to heaven is indeed narrow and straight, and few find it. But each community and each generation contributes its few who dare to walk and struggle alone. And through the revolving ages, the precious ones are being housed in heaven. If you and I miss that happy land, others will shoulder the cross, pass out of the popular way, make the solitary journey, and take our crown which we have so ignobly and foolishly lost.

A city is the symbol of life in its magnificence, perfection, and glory. Heaven will be the realization of all this. In this figure of a city is found the closeness of the sympathy, love, and fellowship that will abound there.

Along transparent glassy streets
Their Holy feet do stray,
In Companies of perfect joy,
With Christ to light their way.

Celestial city, Happy land!
The home of Saints at rest,
Contented in eternal bliss,
To Love and to be blessed!

Chapter 4

LIFE IN THE CONTINUING CITY

"For here we have no continuing city, but we seek one to come"—Hebrews 13:14.

The inconstant, fleeting nature of earth's most substantial and social things is proverbial. Poetry and fiction speak of it. It is part of the sad experience of life, and the hastiest observation confirms that earth is prone to change. Its fairest flowers fade away, and its most precious joys soon wither. But heaven is enduring. It is not the pilgrim's inn. It is home; it abides and is settled forever.

Heaven is a *prepared city;* it is ready and complete. (See Hebrews 11:16.) Homes are already built, and no strenuous labor faces us. Everything is ready, anticipated, and furnished by a knowledge and ability that knows all our needs and stops at no expense.

It is a *holy city* where nothing impure can enter. (See Revelation 11:2.) Everything is as brilliant and pure as a diamond. It is great in its goodness and light, great in its attractive power, and great in frame, beauty, and grandeur. Everything about the city is precious in value and costly in richness.

That it is a holy city is more to our purpose and for our good than its greatness. The term "holy" baffles the critics to define with certainty and clearness. It certainly means separated and devoted to God. It certainly means purity. Earthly cities are great, but their purity is often opposite their greatness. In heaven greatness is never divorced from goodness. Not so on earth. Heaven is a city whose purity clarifies its atmosphere and causes it to sparkle and glitter like crystal. Its light is in its purity, and its brightness and permanency are emanated from God and the Lamb.

Manifestations Of Glory

"And there came unto me one of the seven angels which had the seven vials full of the seven last plagues, and talked with me, saying, Come hither, I will shew thee the bride, the Lamb's wife. And he carried me away in the spirit to a great and high mountain, and shewed me that great city, the holy Jerusalem, descending out of heaven from God, Having the glory of God: and her light was like unto a stone most precious, even like a jasper stone, clear as crystal; And had a wall great and high" (Revelation 21:9-12).

It took the light and power of the Spirit and the perspective of a mountain top to view this city in its magnificence and glory. What grandeur in the vision, the ecstasy of the spirit, the entrancing city, and the inspiration of the great and high mountains! All these heightened and made the view ravishing but could transfer only a faint resemblance to the reality. It is a picture of exquisite and fadeless beauty but a picture only. No inspired trance or lofty mountain view could portray the life, reality, and substance of heaven.

The revelation of God is this glory; and it forms the light, blessedness, and splendor of the city. The glory of God constitutes the loveliness and glory of the land. The opulence and wealth of its life! Her light was like a precious stone. God's glory the sun! The light coming from such a sun would dazzle and flame like earth's most costly, beautiful, bright, and sparkling diamond.

Surrounded By Strength And Beauty

The walls and gates of heaven find their expressive significance in Isaiah: "Thou shalt call thy walls salvation, and thy gates praise." "Behold I will lay thy stones with fair colors and lay thy foundations with sapphires. And I will make thy windows of agates and thy gates of carbuncles and all thy borders of pleasant stones." We have a strong city: "Salvation will God appoint for walls and bulwarks" (Isaiah 60:18; 54:11-12; 26:1).

The walls represent the strength and power of salvation to heavenly life. So mighty are the forces of their salvation in heaven that consideration of them fills the believer with transporting rapture and energy: "After this I beheld, and, lo, a great multitude, which no man could number, of all nations, and kindreds, and people, and tongues, stood before the throne, and before the Lamb, clothed with white robes, and palms in their hands; And cried with a loud voice, saying, Salvation to our God which sitteth upon the throne, and unto the Lamb. And all the angels stood round about the throne, and about the elders and the four beasts, and fell before the throne on their faces, and worshipped God, Saying, Amen: Blessing, and glory, and wisdom, and thanksgiving, and honor, and power, and might, be unto our God for ever and ever. Amen" (Revelation 7:9-12).

The hope of salvation ought to be joyous, glorious, and hope-inspiring to us on earth. No matter what it means to us, however, it means more to those already in heaven. We have the brook, and they have its ocean streams; we have the glitter and mildness of its starlight, but they have the sun's unclouded strength.

The wall is great and high: "And the wall of the city had twelve foundations, and in them the names of the twelve apostles of the Lamb. . . .And the building of the wall of it was of jasper: and the city was pure gold, like unto clear glass. And the foundations of the wall of the city were garnished with all manner of precious stones" (Revelation 21:14, 18-19).

The walls are for protection. Twelve foundations indicate strength, while jewels represent beauty and preciousness. The heavenly life will be a protected life, walled in by jeweled beauty. The motives and influences that hold us to heaven will be strong, but not dull and heavy. The walls are jasper, and all the twelve foundations are gemmed with every variety of precious stones.

We have in the fourth chapter this description of God: "And immediately I was in the Spirit: and, behold, a throne was set in heaven, and one sat on the throne. And he that sat was to look upon like a jasper and a sardine stone" (Revelation 4:2-3). How remarkable are the walls of the heavenly city, made out of the same material! How closely God and His city are allied and unified!

This same book says: "Him that overcometh will I make a pillar in the temple of my God, and he shall go no more out: and I will write upon him the name of my God, and the name of the city of my God, which is new Jerusalem, which cometh down out of heaven from my God: and I will write upon him my new name" (Revelation 3:12).

The city was transparent gold, reflecting every form of beauty, far surpassing any earthly gold in richness, purity, and value. No earthly wealth and loveliness can exceed these! Earthly vocabularies are exhausted, yet only the outside is described. What there is of wealth and good inside defies all language to convey. Diamonds, gold, and jewels are valueless and dull compared to that glorious city.

Praise, Purity, And Power

All these outward adornments, so unparalleled in their value and preciousness, are indicative of the principal joys and pursuits of the heavenly life. Godlike are the persons whose stable and precious characters are represented by twelve jeweled foundations! It is a glorious land whose light and purity glitter like brilliant diamonds and whose society is as flawless and pure as transparent gold.

"Thy gates praise"—the gates are places of counsel, wisdom, adornment, and power. (See Isaiah 60:18.) The gates are of one pearl each. There are twelve of them, each unrivaled in beauty, cost, and purity. They are entrances and impress us with the unity, purity, and worth of all who enter there. Those holy gates forever bar pollution, sin, and shame. The angels have much to do with the entrance into the heavenly gates and with the stay in there. All that is termed kingly, and all that belongs to honor and glory are in that heavenly city.

The very pavement is made of earth's purest gold and mirrors the forms of heavenly saints who walk along its streets. Their forms are too beautiful to rest their shadows on any substance less precious than gold refined and polished to perfection. And those forms are too beautiful not to be reflected and constantly mirrored as they pass along. These forms of perfect beauty add much to the charms of the city.

In this world, death reigns. There, life reigns: "And he shewed me a pure river of water of life, clear as crystal, proceeding out of the throne of God and of the Lamb. In the midst of the street of it, and on either side of the river, was there the tree of life, which bare twelve manner of fruits and yielded her fruit every month: and the leaves of the tree were for the healing of the nations. And there shall be no more curse: but the throne of God and of the Lamb shall be in it; and his servants shall serve him" (Revelation 22:1-3).

Heaven will be life in its full vigor, like a deep river, exhaustless and wide. It will not be a branch or a well but a river, ever expanding and moving on. All things in heaven will be to refresh, gladden, and increase life. Heaven's life flows out of the throne of God.

The Mystery Of The Lamb

Heaven will be the place where God's power will be seen and felt. He will rule with unlimited power and absolute authority. His throne is not separate from the Lamb. The Son of God and His atoning sacrifice unite with the throne to enrich the deep current of heavenly life.

Forever the melody of heaven will go on: "And they sung a new song, saying, Thou art worthy to take the book, and to open the seals thereof: for thou wast slain, and hast redeemed us to God by thy blood out of every kindred, and tongue, and people, and nation; And hast made us unto our God kings and priests: and we shall reign on the earth. And I beheld, and I heard the voice of many angels round about the throne and the beasts and the elders: and the numbers of them was ten thousands times ten thousand, and thousands of thousands; Saying with a loud voice, Worthy is the Lamb that was slain to receive power, and riches, and wisdom, and strength, and honour, and glory, and blessing" (Revelation 5:9-12).

Every new delight and discovery in the heavenly life will be the unfolding of the wonderful mystery and exhaustless power of "the Lamb slain from the foundation of the world" (Revelation 13:8). Everything in heaven will further the vigor, expansion, and glory of that life. The tree of life will give its fruit with freshness, frequency, and energy. Its very leaves are health-giving and invigorating.

All the dire effects of Adam's fall will be removed. No traces of the first man's blasting steps will be seen or felt. The cause of earth's groaning and sighing will be destroyed. Neither the power of Adam nor the dire effects of sin will be there. But the power of God, with all its recreating energy and the power of the cross to redeem, renew, and perfect, will be.

Perfected In Truth

Service of the highest and most adoring form

will characterize heaven. All will be melody and praise, without a discordant note. The inhabitants of heaven will have a perfect vision of God. That vision will be the melody, study, and pursuit of glorified spirits. To know God will be the employment and bliss of heaven. Believers will be sealed for Him with His name on their foreheads. The sign of ownership, loyalty, and consecration to God—without the hands of priest, sacrament, or ceremony—is placed on them. They come to God in person, and from Him they receive all His treasure.

All lesser lights are obscured, and all intermediaries are retired. God and Christ, with all the fullness of their divine and eternal affluence, are in constant contact. The light of God's presence hides and disperses all the feeble lights of earth. God shines with splendor on the glorified ones, and the divine authority of the cross lifts them to royal privileges. They are not only priests but kings to God. Earth has no insight into the glories its inhabitants will be lifted to in heaven. Men have no thought or imagination of the scepter that will be put into the hands of the heirs when their inheritance is received.

Does the vision of John transport and delight us? Then heaven is the place where our thirstings for Him are satisfied and our visions of Him are perfect and glorious.

With sublime and soothing truth, the Bible declares the superiority of the heavenly life.

Heaven robes the saints and transports them with a deathless and painless life. Its length is eternal, and its conditions are absolute. There is the absence of every form of evil and the presence of every form of good. The heavenly home—a crown of glory—is an unspeakable joy!

"And there shall be no more curse: but the throne of God and of the Lamb shall be in it; and his servants shall serve him: And they shall see his face; and his name shall be in their foreheads. And there shall be no night there; and they need no candle, neither light of the sun; for the Lord God giveth them light: and they shall reign for ever and ever" (Revelation 22:3-5).

Interpretations of John's Revelation are almost endless. But as varied as they may be, one thing is sure: the description of the heavenly Jerusalem in its last chapters is a pattern after which the earthly is to be shaped.

Moses' tabernacle was patterned in the heavenlies. The Jew who studied and followed the pattern understood the principles and substance of the original. The third heaven, where God abides in His unveiled glory, was described by John and presented as the model for God's work on earth. We study this picture of the heavenly to know what heaven is.

To that Jerusalem above
With singing I repair;
While in the flesh, my hope and love,

My heart and soul, are there:
There my exalted Saviour stands,
My merciful High Priest,
And still extends his wounded hands,
To take me to his breast—Charles Wesley.

Chapter 5

KINGDOM, CROWN, AND INHERITANCE

"Happy will I be and forever happy, if after death I might hear the melody of those hymns and hallelujahs which the citizens of that celestial kingdom and the squadron of those blessed spirits sing in praise of the eternal king. This is that sweet music which St. John heard in the Revelation, when the inhabitants of heaven sang, 'Let all the world bless thee, O Lord.' To Thee be given all honor and dominion for a world of worlds—Amen"—Jeremy Taylor.

What magnificence and splendor exist in a kingdom! What ambitions result from the desire to possess a kingdom! Heaven must be won as a kingdom is won and must be struggled for as a kingdom is struggled for. Heaven stimulates as a kingdom stimulates.

The work of grace occurs in the human heart, called the kingdom of grace. Heaven is the kingdom of glory. "Come ye blessed of my Father, inherit the kingdom prepared for you" (Matthew

25:34) are the words of Jesus as He rewards the honored ones on His right hand in the day of judgment.

"That ye would walk worthy of God, who hath called you unto his kingdom and glory," warns Paul (1 Thessalonians 2:12). Here we have a combination of kingdom and glory. What a magnificent combination! "Rich in faith, and heirs of the kingdom," says James (James 2:5). "For so an entrance shall be ministered unto you abundantly into the everlasting kingdom of our Lord and Saviour Jesus Christ," declares Peter (2 Peter 1:11).

The Bible declares future life will be a throne: "To him that overcometh will I grant to sit with me in my throne, even as I also overcame, and am set down with my Father in his throne" (Revelation 3:21).

Our Eternal Rewards

It is a crown: "Hold fast that thou hast, that no man take thy crown" (Revelation 3:11). An incorruptible crown, its glory never dims and its power never abates. Paul spoke of the Isthmian runners and their strenuous self-denial and vigorous efforts. "Now they do it to obtain a corruptible crown; but we an incorruptible" (1 Corinthians 9:25).

Paul declared at the very point of death: "Henceforth there is laid up for me a crown of righteousness, which the Lord, the righteous judge, shall give me at that day: and not to me only, but unto all them also that love his appearing" (2 Timothy 4:8). "A crown of righteousness," awarded according to rigid demands of integrity. "Blessed," says James, "is the man that endureth temptation: for when he is tried, he shall receive the crown of life, which the Lord hath promised to them that love him" (James 1:12).

Peter declared, "And when the chief Shepherd shall appear, ye shall receive a crown of glory that fadeth not away" (1 Peter 5:4). How this stimulates us to temperance and self-denial!

"Know ye not that they which run in a race run all, but one receiveth the prize? So run, that ye may obtain. And every man that striveth for the mastery is temperate in all things. Now they do it to obtain a corruptible crown; but we an incorruptible. I therefore so run, not as uncertainly; so fight I, not as one that beateth the air: But I keep under my body, and bring it into subjection: lest that by any means, when I have preached to others, I myself should be a castaway" (1 Corinthians 9:24-27).

This was the effect of this incorruptible crown on the chief of the apostles.

How grand the awards of eternity are! Glory, a kingdom, authority, and grandeur are in it! A crown belongs to kingly heads, conquerors, and heroes. Kingship belongs to it. Overcomers and conquerors enter the realms of life. How greatly were Grecian athletes stimulated by a perishable crown! They would endure any toil to win them.

The spectators of their contest, the judge, and the crown are all presented as examples for us in our contest for heaven.

Heirs Of The King

Revelation proclaims a sweeping declaration of heirship: "He that overcometh shall inherit all things; and I will be his God, and he shall be my son" (Revelation 21:7).

Colossians describes a combination of reward and inheritance: "Knowing that of the Lord ye shall receive the reward of the inheritance: for ye serve the Lord Christ" (Colossians 3:24).

Heaven is called an *inheritance*. It comes by relationship and heirship: "For ye have not received the spirit of bondage again to fear; but ye have received the spirit of adoption, whereby we cry, Abba, Father. The spirit itself beareth witness with our spirit, that we are the children of God: And if children, then heirs; heirs of God, and joint heirs with Christ; if so be that we suffer with him, that we may be also glorified together" (Romans 8:15-17). Galatians 4:6-7 states, "And because ye are sons, God hath sent forth the spirit of his Son into your hearts, crying, Abba, Father. Wherefore thou art no more a servant, but a son; and if a son, then an heir of God through Christ."

Peter has a magnificent statement of the heirship and inheritance of saints in heaven: "Blessed be the God and Father of our Lord Jesus Christ, which according to his abundant mercy hath begotten us again unto a lively hope by the resurrection of Jesus Christ from the dead, To an inheritance incorruptible, and undefiled, and that fadeth not away, reserved in heaven for you, Who are kept by the power of God through faith unto salvation" (1 Peter 1:3-5).

It is represented as a gift: "The gift of God is eternal life" (Romans 6:23). These rich and diverse expressions portray heaven as a great *reward*. It is seen as an imperishable *inheritance* of fadeless beauty, a great *prize,* and an unspeakable and indescribable *gift*. Heaven's inspiration has produced the saintliest saints, the most heroic heroes, the greatest conquerors, and the most self-denying servants.

How strong are the stimulating forces that heaven awakens! If we meditated on the joys of heaven, we could not dispense with the deepest conviction, the most ardent faith, and the firmest loyalty. These heavenly thoughts strengthen our weakness, disperse our depression, and brighten our darkness. They call us to purity and nobleness and awaken us to righteousness.

Thoughts of heaven quicken our faith. Our only sure and solid foundation is the hope of heaven. The only solution to earth's mysteries, the only righter of earth's wrongs, and the only cure for worldliness, is heaven. We need an infusion of heaven into our faith and hope that will create a homesickness for that blessed place. God's home is heaven. Eternal life and all good were born there and flourish there. All life, happiness, beauty, and glory are native to the home of God.

All this belongs to and awaits the heirs of God in heaven. What a glorious inheritance!

'Tis God's all-animating voice
That calls thee from on high;
'Tis his own hand presents the prize
To thine aspiring eye—

That prize, with peerless glories bright,
Which shall new luster boast,
When victors' wreaths and monarchs' gems
Shall blend in common dust.

Blest Saviour, introduced by thee,
Have I my race begun;
And, crowned with victory, at thy feet
I'll lay my honors down—Philip Doddridge.

Chapter 6

PARADISE AND ETERNAL LIFE

"Go on and faint not. Something of yours is in heaven other than the flesh of your exalted Saviour. . . . You must grow out of your shell and live, triumph, reign, and be more than a conqueror. For your Captain is more than a conqueror, and He makes you partaker of His conquest and victory"—Samuel Rutherford.

The word "paradise" is used by Paul as equivalent to the third heaven—the abode of God. It is also used in Revelation: "To him that overcometh will I give to eat of the tree of life, which is in the midst of the paradise of God" (Revelation 2:7).

Paradise is separated, distinguished, and emphasized as a marked and distinct place. It is the beautiful abode of God and angelic beings where true Christians will be taken after death. How unparalleled in every excellence, dignity, and loveliness paradise must be! To that gracious home the thief was translated *the same day* the jeering and infuriated mob crucified him with Jesus so his cross would defame that of the Son of God. But instead of increasing the ignominy and shame of Jesus, it added luster and power to the cross by lifting a robber from shame and guilt to the glorious beauties of heaven! The words "To day shalt thou be with me in paradise" have given hope of immortality to many a sinner as he has lifted his prayerful, dying eyes and said, "Remember me" (Luke 23:42-43).

Heaven is a place of beauty and purity; but sinful robbers, washed in the blood, also go there. *"With me"*—what exalted glory, supreme dignity, and divine companionship for a thief! How infinite the condescension of Jesus to share His glory and joy with him! One of the noblest memorials to the death of Jesus is that thief lifted from a cross of guilt to a throne of glory. The wonders of that death! What tongue can tell of its marvels? But "To day shalt thou be with me in paradise" is only the beginning.

Resurrected To Life

In the notable conversation with Nicodemus, Jesus elevated all who would believe in Him to the position of "eternal life."

"And as Moses lifted up the serpent in the wilderness, even so must the Son of man be lifted up: That whosoever believeth in him should not perish, but have eternal life. For God so loved the world, that he gave his only begotten son, that whosoever believeth in him should not perish, but have everlasting life" (John 3:14-16).

Again, in the fourth chapter, the eternal glory is designated as eternal life; it is the harvest of our faithful sowing and tilling in this life. "And he that reapeth receiveth wages, and gathereth fruit unto life eternal: that both he that soweth and he that reapeth may rejoice together" (John 4:36).

The resurrection is unto life: "Marvel not at this: for the hour is coming, in the which all that are in the graves shall hear his voice, And shall come forth; they that have done good, unto the resurrection of life; and they that have done evil, unto the resurrection of damnation" (John 5:28-29).

That wonderful saying to Martha is the declaration of the great truth that the crowning glory of the future is eternal life: "Jesus said unto her, Thy brother shall rise again. Martha saith unto him, I know that he shall rise again in the resurrection at the last day. Jesus said unto her, I am the resurrection, and the life: he that believeth in me, though he were dead, yet shall he live: And whosoever liveth and believeth in me shall never die. Believest thou this? She said unto him, Yea, Lord: I believe that thou art the Christ, the Son of God, which should come into the world" (John 11:23-27).

We also hear Jesus say: "He that loveth his life shall lose it; and he that hateth his life in this world shall keep it unto life eternal" (John 12:25).

Jesus gave His disciples a magnificent, comforting promise just before His death, while the gloom of Gethsemane and Calvary was on them: "Let not your heart be troubled: ye believe in God, believe also in me. In my Father's house are many mansions: if it were not so, I would have told you. I go to prepare a place for you. And if I go and prepare a place for you, I will come again, and receive you unto myself; that where I am, there ye may be also" (John 14:1-3).

Dwelling In His Presence

Heaven will relieve all the troubles of this life. Every earthly pain will be eased, all fiery trials quenched, and all tears dried. Jesus said heaven is a place: "I go to prepare a *place* for you. If I go and prepare a *place* for you. . .where I am"—Jesus is located in heaven. Somewhere in God's house of many mansions Jesus sits upon His throne and manifests His glory. There, with their exalted Lord, His saints dwell in eternal, unalloyed good. We not only see the purpose and inflexible decree of Jesus to have us in His Father's house but also the longings of His heart: "Where I am, there ye may be also."

This comes out most fully in His high priestly prayer: "Father, I will that they also, whom thou hast given me, be with me where I am; that they may behold my glory, which thou hast given me" (John 17:24). That Jesus wants us with Him is not a mere sentiment to adorn or sweeten but a declared, operative, and eternal decree—"Father I *will.*" His heart and authority are in it.

"Having a desire to depart, and to be with Christ; which is far better," says Paul in Philippians 1:23. To be in heaven is to be with Christ.

Jesus has gone to heaven "to appear in the presence of God for us" (Hebrews 9:24). By the mystery of His death and the glory of His intercession, He is preparing a place for us and preparing us for the place.

Jesus is exalted in heaven at the right hand of the throne of God. The throne is the symbol of power; and the direction of the right hand is the symbol of honor, glory, and majesty. Jesus is exalted to the highest place in heaven to which God's power can raise Him. The apostle declares the exalted dignity of Jesus: "According to the working of his mighty power, which he wrought in Christ, when he raised him from the dead, and set him at his own right hand in the heavenly places, Far above all principality, and power, and might, and dominion, and every name that is named, not only in this world, but also in that which is to come: And hath put all things under his feet, and gave him to be the head over all things to the church, Which is his body, the fullness of him that filleth all in all" (Ephesians 1:19-23).

The highest position of legal glory is His, and we are to be partners with Him in all the splendors of the eternal world. With divine magnificence

God crowns, exalts, and glorifies Jesus! And with the same exhaustless generosity and magnificence the Son dispenses the boundless wealth of heaven to His glorified ones.

Comforted By The Shepherd

What Jesus has done for us here in His startling advent and unparalleled humiliation and suffering is the true mirror of the wonderful things He will do for us in the other world. But it is only a faint reflection of them. For His ability is greatly increased, and the conditions are far more favorable in heaven than they were when under the limitations that chained Him here.

Of one thing we are constantly reminded: Jesus will be with us and will serve us like a shepherd feeding his flock on the richest food of heaven, leading us to new and living fountains of bliss, knowledge, and light. To have Jesus with us will be the peak and sum of all happiness, perfection, and good. What beauty in His face! What wealth untold in His character! Only eternity can unfold His unbounded resources.

What matchless and indescribable charms He has for those who are possessed by His love. While in prison, the gifted and saintly Samuel Rutherford used his great gifts to speak of Jesus and His loveliness: "I never believed till now that there was so much to be found in Christ on this side of death and heaven. Oh, the ravishments of heavenly joy which may be had here, in the small gleanings and comforts that fall from Christ."

If Jesus was so much to the gifted and holy Samuel Rutherford, while banished and a prisoner, what must He be to those in heaven? What beauties there must be in the unfoldings of His character to the glorified! What a heaven it must be! It cannot be said too strongly that *we are bound to love heaven for Jesus' sake*. We are bound to long for heaven because Jesus is there. We are bound to be filled with joy when the hour comes to go there, because it is the hour to see Jesus, meet Jesus, and enjoy being with Him forever.

O Paradise, O Paradise,
Who doth not crave for rest?
Who would not seek the happy land
Where they that loved are blest;

Where loyal hearts and true,
Stand ever in the light,
All rapture, through and through
In God's most holy sight?

O Paradise! O Paradise!
The world is growing old;
Who would not be at rest and free
Where love is never cold?

Chapter 7

The Brilliance Of Eternal Life

"Mr. Valiant said, 'I am going to my Father's and though with great difficulty I got hither yet now I do not repent me of all the trouble I have been at to arrive where I am.' When the day that he must go over was come many accompanied him to the riverside, into which as he went he said, 'Death, where is thy sting? Grave, where is thy victory?' So he passed over, and all the trumpets sounded for him on the other side"—John Bunyan.

The Bible makes much use of the term *life* as the central and fundamental idea of heaven and its enjoyments, employments, and character. The term is almost too literal to be reckoned as a symbol. It is a comprehensive symbol, and its nearness to the literal enhances its value as a symbol.

The New Testament abounds in the use of this symbol. It is the result of the gospel. Faith plants the seed of eternal life, and it grows in the faithful heart through all the struggles and years of this life. It finds its eternal unfolding in fullest expansion and abundance in heaven. "As many as were ordained to eternal life" (Acts 13:48).

"To them who by patient continuance in well doing seek for glory and honor and immortality, eternal life" (Romans 2:7).

"That as sin hath reigned unto death, even so might grace reign through righteousness unto eternal life by Jesus Christ our Lord" (Romans 5:21).

"To reign in life" means this: "But now being made free from sin, and become servants to God, ye have your fruit unto holiness, and the end everlasting life. For the wages of sin is death; but the gift of God is eternal life through Jesus Christ our Lord" (Romans 6:22-23).

Anticipating Heaven

Paul, in giving the reason why the true Christian groans to enter into heaven, says, "For we that are in this tabernacle do groan, being burdened: not for that we would be unclothed, but clothed upon, that mortality might be swallowed up of life" (2 Corinthians 5:4).

To Timothy, Paul says, "Lay hold on eternal life, whereunto thou art also called" (1 Timothy 6:12). He exhorts the rich in this way: "That they do good, that they be rich in good works, ready to distribute, willing to communicate; Laying up in store for themselves a good foundation against the time to come, that they may lay hold on eternal life" (1 Timothy 6:18-19).

James designates heaven as a "crown of life" (James 1:7). It is called "the resurrection of life" (John 5:29). The statements of the apostles and Christ imply that eternal life is freedom from opposition to death. In the term *life* is concentrated every good that man can desire to enjoy. Heaven is the possession of the first and last blessing of man. It is the essence of all happiness. Life is the state and affluence of heaven—immortal and undecayed with no liability to deteriorate. The state of the heavenly world *is* life. Its book is the Book of Life; its river is the river of life; its tree is the tree of life; and its water is the water of life.

The young man who came to Jesus asked, "What shall I do to inherit eternal life?" (Luke 18:18). What a divine gift this life is! It is bounded by the cradle, the symbol of helplessness, and by death, dark and painful. Hampered by sickness and marred by distress, we cling to and at last surrender it only in a despairing or triumphant struggle.

Life In Its Fullest

But eternal life involves the untold, unimagined, and brilliant glories of heaven! What measureless wealth! What deathless raptures! The most exalted strains of music would be discord to the harmony of heaven, and the brightest vision would turn into the darkest midnight! Summer suns would chill like the ice of December when contrasted with the splendor of its nightless day. The sweetest poetry on earth would be dull prose in heaven.

What is eternal life? Who can dream or imagine that life? *Heaven has it*! It will be the surprise of the saints as they leave earth and pass through the gates of the celestial city.

Jesus will lead the heavenly inhabitants to "fountains of living waters" (Revelation 7:17). Here is a life that refreshes, blesses, and satisfies the soul as water refreshes, blesses, and satisfies the body. Here is a constant unfolding of life, full and overflowing like a fountain.

Heaven will be the pursuit, enjoyment, and increase of life. It will be eternal. Life in heaven will be a rapture. Mind, soul, and spirit will be widened, elevated, deepened, refined, and beautified by it. Everything will conspire to make the life supremely blessed and glorious. Christ will feed that life on the richest pastures and lead the way to fountains of living water. "God will wipe away all tears" from the eyes of that life. (See Revelation 7:17; 21:4.)

The heavens shall glow with splendor,
But brighter far than they
The saints shall shine in glory,
As Christ shall them array:
The beauty of the Saviour,
Shall dazzle every eye,
In the crowning day that's coming by and by.

Our pain shall then be over,
We'll sin and sigh no more;
Behind us all of sorrow,
And naught but joy before,
A joy in our Redeemer,
As we to him are nigh,
In the crowning day that's coming by and by.

Chapter 8

THE PROMISE OF HEAVEN

"The eye of flesh is not capable of seeing, nor the ear of hearing, nor the heart of understanding heaven and its glories. But there the eye, the ear, and the heart are made capable. How else could we enjoy those things in heaven? The more perfect the sight, the more delightful will be the beautiful object. The more perfect the appetite, the sweeter the food; the more musical the ear, the more pleasant the melody, and the more perfect the soul, the more joyous these joys, and the more glorious these glories"—Richard Baxter.

The Holy Spirit is said to be the earnest in heaven. The "earnest" is the security and foretaste, and so the Holy Spirit is the certainty of heaven. He puts the fact, taste, power, and ambition for heaven strongly and constantly in our hearts. The refrain and chorus are, "Heaven is my home."

"In whom ye also trusted, after that ye heard the word of truth, the gospel of your salvation: in whom also after that ye believed, ye were sealed with that holy Spirit of promise, Which is the earnest of our inheritance until the redemption of the purchased possession, unto the praise of his glory" (Ephesians 1:13-14).

"Now he which stablisheth us with you in Christ, and hath annointed us, is God; Who hath also sealed us, and given the earnest of the Spirit in our hearts" (2 Corinthians 1:21-22).

These great texts present to us the ministry and work of the Holy Spirit as He forms in us the fact and experience of heaven. He shapes us in desire and heavenliness at every point.

Thirsting For Heaven

The music and hope of heaven would fill and sweeten our lives if we lived in the full power of the Spirit. His power settles our faith and quickens the sentiment about heaven. By the Spirit's mighty workings, heaven becomes a sublime and glorious fact. The power of the Holy Spirit puts in us a thirst for heaven. He gives us constant tastes and visions of heaven, until all other tastes pall and all other visions are heavy and dull. He gives us notes of its harmony and all earth's notes are discord. The power of the Spirit binds us to heaven because Jesus is its center and glory.

Strongly and insistently, the Holy Spirit uses heaven and its manifold good to move saints to action. The Holy Spirit implants heaven in us. The

Holy Spirit Himself, given to us, is God's mark of ownership and security. His authority is put on us.

But it is not His sealing process—its condition, significance, or results in full—that we now consider but the *earnest* of future and eternal things. The Holy Spirit is the earnest of heaven to us. "Earnest" means the pledge that is given so the contract will be faithfully and fully carried out. An earnest is part of the thing itself, given as a security that the whole will be given in its time. Through the Holy Spirit, God gives us a part of heaven as a pledge of the full heaven when the time is ripe. The Holy Spirit is both a foretaste and a pledge of heaven.

The Holy Spirit puts heaven in us when He puts Himself in us. All our tastes, struggles, and longings for heaven are the creations of His power and the sure tests of His presence. If there is no heavenly spirit and no heavenly yearning in us, then there is no Holy Spirit in us. God prepares us for heaven by the Holy Spirit and plants in us the heavenly mind and image. The indwelling Spirit of God makes us unlike earth and like heaven. The Holy Spirit matures hope to its brightest luster and enables the saint to "glory in tribulation" and "rejoice in hope of the glory of God" (Romans 5:2-3).

Pressing On Toward Heaven

Paul, by the Spirit, promoted heaven. In mid-career, fastened to life and earth by his strenuous toil, he paused and recorded his loyalty to heaven and to Jesus. In Paul's estimation, and in every true estimate, they are one. "I am in a strait betwixt two, having a desire to depart, and be with Christ; which is far better" (Philippians 1:23). On his stretch for heaven, he says, "We are confident, I say, and willing rather to be absent from the body, and to be present with the Lord" (2 Corinthians 5:8).

Paul is ever pressing on: "Forgetting those things which are behind, and reaching forth unto those things which are before, I press toward the mark for the prize of the high calling of God in Christ Jesus" (Philippians 3:13-14). He is always keeping his body under subjection, so that he won't lose the incorruptible crown. (See 1 Corinthians 9:37.) At the close of his good battle, heaven is still in full view, with its crown gleaming brighter under Nero's axe. It is the thought, hope, and fact of heaven that forms Christian character and matures it into unearthly beauty and perfection.

The stringent demands of entering into eternal life could not be described more acutely than by Jesus Christ: "And if thy hand offend thee, cut it off: it is better for thee to enter into life maimed, then having two hands to go into hell, into the fire that never shall be quenched" (Mark 9:43).

Heaven is a reward. "Great is your reward in heaven" (Matthew 5:12), says Christ to His persecuted and reviled disciples. "And, behold, I come

67

quickly; and my reward is with me, to give every man according as his work shall be" (Revelation 22:12). The meaning of reward is dues paid for work. "For the Son of man shall come in the glory of his Father with his angels; and then he shall reward every man according to his works" (Matthew 16:27).

Then let the wildest storms arise;
Let tempest mingle earth and skies;
No fatal shipwrecks shall I fear,
But all my treasures with me bear.

If thou, my Jesus, still be nigh,
Cheerful I live, and joyful die;
Secure, when mortal comforts flee,
To find ten thousand worlds in thee
—Philip Doddridge.

Chapter 9

THE STATE OF HEAVEN

"And I heard as it were the voice of a great multitude. . .saying, Alleluia: for the Lord God omnipotent reigneth. Let us be glad and rejoice, and give honour to him: for the marriage of the Lamb is come, and his wife hath made herself ready"—Revelation 19:6-7.

Heaven is a state as well as a place. However fascinating the outward appearance may be to eye or ear, how pleasing to taste or touch, or how ecstatic to feeling all the scenes and sounds, these are not the prime sources of its attraction. It is *a state*—a state of enthronement, elevation, and freedom. Much has been left behind of the old, the worn out, and the burdensome; and much of the new, the strange, and the wonderful will be there. It will be a state of *perfected knowledge*. Then we shall know even as we are known. God knows us perfectly here. We will know Him and all things perfectly there.

"For we know in part, and we prophesy in part.

But when that which is perfect is come, then that which is in part shall be done away. When I was a child, I spake as a child, I understood as a child, I thought as a child: but when I became a man, I put away childish things. For now we see through a glass, darkly; but then face to face: now I know in part, but then shall I know even as also I am known" (1 Corinthians 13:9-12).

Imagine the unspeakable benefits in a state where we know all things perfectly! There will be neither height nor depth nor breadth nor length, in heaven, earth, or hell, that will not lie open to our knowledge in that exalted and perfected state. All mysteries will be gone.

Freed From Sin

In Romans we have a statement vital to heaven: "But now being made free from sin, and become servants to God, ye have your fruit unto holiness, and the end everlasting life" (Romans 6:22). To "make free" is *to emancipate*. A dual action is seen here—emancipation from sin and enslavement to God. These bear the fruit of holiness if they are found in a heart where God reigns, and heaven belongs to such characters by inheritance.

Two questions constantly arise from those who are heaven-bound: How free can I be from sin? How thoroughly devoted to God can I be? These questions have engaged and perplexed the holiest of men. Too much time and thought have been spent by men trying to fix the limits by theoretical statements. The Scriptures make strong affirmations at this point. An elder in Burmah says, "I find on reading the apostles' writings that they address their fellow Christians and speak of themselves as persons that are dead to sin, buried with Christ into death. They are dead, and their lives are hid with Christ in God. They have crucified the flesh with its affections and lusts. Their old man is crucified with Christ. They are dead to sin by consequence and are freed from sin. Being born of God, they have overcome the world; the world is crucified to them, and they are crucified to the world."

"Now these things are mentioned not only as things to be desired or sought after, but as already obtained. 'Ye are dead—have crucified the flesh—have put off the old man—are freed from sin—hath ceased from sin'" (Galatians 5:24; Colossians 3:9; Romans 5:7; 1 Peter 4:1).

How many people before and since have raised the same questions? Of one thing we may be sure: the experience and attitude of Christian attainment and obtainment set forth in the New Testament is open to all Christians of every age and place.

Books on holiness may give us no light, and theories may only confuse us. But with our open Bibles, prayer, and the increasing light and power of the Holy Spirit, each can settle the question as a personal experience. We must keep this divine statement ever before our minds: "But now being made free from sin, and become servants to God

ye have your fruit unto holiness" (Romans 6:22).
This is complete freedom from sin and enslavement to God, with the full possibilities of God's grace, Christ's blood, the power of the Holy Spirit, and faith.

Our All In All

God is "able to do exceeding abundantly above all that we ask or think" (Ephesians 3:20). "All things are possible to him that believeth" (Mark 9:23). "He that spared not his own Son, but delivered him up for us all, how shall he not with him also freely give us all things?" (Romans 8:32).

God has given us all things in Christ—that by prayer we can have all that there is in Christ—and we are charged to "be filled with all the fullness of God" (Ephesians 3:19). He is able to make us abound in all grace, that we "always having all sufficiency in all things, may abound to every good work" (2 Corinthians 9:8). God can "make you perfect in every good work to do his will, working in you that which is well pleasing in his sight" (Hebrews 13:21). Then we "may stand perfect and complete in all the will of God" (Colossians 4:12). These wonderful Scriptures concerning grace fully answer the question as to how free we can be from sin and how thoroughly we can be devoted to God.

This "fruit unto holiness" (Romans 6:22) is absolutely necessary as a prerequisite for heaven. Without holiness no man will see the Lord. (See

72

Hebrews 12:14.) Holiness is an imperative, inflexible, eternal condition of heaven. A holy God demands holiness among men as well as angels. "Every man that striveth for the mastery is temperate in all things. They do it to obtain a corruptible crown; but we an incorruptible. I therefore so run, not as uncertainly; so fight I, not as one that beateth the air: But I keep under my body, and bring it into subjection: lest that by any means, when I have preached to others, I myself should be a castaway" (1 Corinthians 9:25-27).

The heavenly virtue stressed here is temperance, the strong master of self under the law of strict self-denial. The apostle enforces the necessity of temperance by referring to athletes who spent much time in training, denying themselves those things they ordinarily indulged in.

The apostle is writing about heaven, and the presence of this temperance is not only to be exercised in the higher realms of man's nature but in the Christian's bodily appetites. Not only is temperance necessary to *become* a Christian, but its daily and hourly exercise are necessary to *continue* as a Christian. "I keep under my body" (1 Corinthians 9:27) means to strike heavily in the face, to render black and blue a hard subject, and to reduce it to self-control and bring the body into subjection. The body is the adversary. It is the seat of self-indulgence which opens the door for Satan's temptations.

Through self-control, pride and self-seeking

appetites restrained and broken. The flesh and spirit are brought under the law of this heavenly race. No one is free from this law. The apostle declared, "if a man also strive for masteries, yet he is not crowned, except he strive lawfully" (2 Timothy 2:5). After the race the winners were examined to see if they had won by lawful means. If they had not, they were deprived of the prize. The law for heavenly contestants is severe self-control. Without it all seeming success in the heavenly race will be rejected.

Rejoicing In Redemption

Heaven makes redemption full, the possession perfect, and the pledge sure. Even here we have the foretaste of the full heaven. Heaven is joy unmixed, eternal, and rapturous. By the presence of the Holy Spirit, we have "joy unspeakable and full of glory" (1 Peter 1:8). While we are still on earth, we "rejoice evermore" (1 Thessalonians 5:16).

To rejoice is the command of earth as well as the luxury of heaven. Heaven is the place and state of perfect rest, but even here peace reigns by the Holy Spirit. "The peace of God, which passeth all understanding, shall keep your hearts and minds through Christ Jesus" (Philippians 4:7). This is the type and beginning of heaven's peace. The Kingdom of God in this world creates "righteousness, and peace, and joy in the Holy Ghost" (Romans 14:17). The Kingdom of God in the next world will create the *perfection* of righteousness, peace, and joy.

"The redemption of the purchased possession" is changed in the Revised Version to, "Unto the redemption of God's own possession" (Ephesians 1:14). God takes possession of us by the Holy Spirit through redemption. By yielding ourselves to be filled, possessed, controlled, and owned by God, He has unlimited authority over us and supreme unmixed control in us. Heaven will give us the fullest possession of God, and heaven will give God the fullest possession of us. But heaven is only for those who are God's possession here.

God's Word reveals another land where the misfortune of poverty and the curse of crime never come, where a life of poverty and a death of the cross puts no mark on the brow. Heaven is made up of earth's banished outlaws.

Scripture gives a description of characters that will be found in heaven: "And others had trial of cruel mockings and scourgings, yea, moreover of bonds and imprisonment: They were stoned, they were sawn asunder, were tempted, were slain with the sword: they wandered about in sheepskins and goatskins; being destitute, afflicted, tormented; (of whom the world was not worthy:) they wandered in deserts, and in mountains, and in dens and caves of the earth" (Hebrews 11:36-38).

Wonderful grace develops saints, while immortals of earth become defamed and ostracized!

The beggar Lazarus and all holy beggars have learned by their begging the secret of faith. They have a heart for heaven! What wonderful companionship and association for our adorable and divine Lord was the thief banned to the cross by earthly justice! Heaven makes redeemed and glorious ones out of the refuse of earth! To add to the glory of Himself and the renown of Abraham, God makes Lazarus, earth's banished one, His own companion! False reputations and earthly rewards are reversed and rectified in Christ's heaven!

In the parable of the rich man and Lazarus, Jesus teaches not only about heaven but also about sad and alarming lessons of hell. All men do not go to heaven. It is *possible* for all men to go to heaven, but all will not. This we learn from the rich man, who, in hell, lifted up his eyes in torment. Heaven is not subjected to the financial and social influences of this world. Lazarus has committed the unpardonable crime of earth—being a beggar. He is scorned, friendless, and buried without tears.

But heaven received Lazarus, the beggar on earth, into more than a kingly society; angels became his attendants, and he became the bosom friend and associate of Abraham, the "friend of God." The heavenly society is not based on money. Purity of character reigns in heaven but money does not.

Everlasting Delight

The favorite Bible word used to describe heaven

is "glory." It means splendor, brightness, magnificence, excellence, dignity, and majesty in the sense of absolute perfection.

Heaven will be a *happy* state. Glory, brilliance, and splendor will bring calm to the breast and joy to the heart. Supreme happiness, with nothing to shadow its brightness, bring pain, or cause sorrow, is promised to the Christian.

Real joys exist in heaven. We do not understand their fullness, but we know listlessness and weariness cannot prevail. Activity is the first and strongest impression given to us of heaven, an activity too intense and profound to be joyless. Their joys are of the highest and most engaging order, filling the heart, mind, and spirit.

We can, perhaps, appreciate more readily its joys by a negative statement rather than the positive and by the ills we will escape rather than by the joys we will inherit.

No sickness—what an immeasurable bliss! No pain—what endless comfort and ease! No sorrow, no cloud, no night, no weariness, no bitterness, no anguish, no penitence, no remorse, no sighs, no tears, no sad laments, no broken hearts, no deathbed scenes, and no dying will be there. We will never find a corpse, a coffin, a hearse, or a grave in all that happy, blissful land. No funeral crowd will ever weep, and no sorrowing one will ever pass through its streets or walk along its cloudless highways. Not only is there an absence of these things, which by their absence is enough to form a delightful heaven—but there is positive good, fullness of joy, and pleasure forevermore. (See Psalm 16:11.)

No chilling winds, or poisonous breath,
Can reach that healthful shore;
Sickness and sorrow, pain and death,
Are felt and feared no more.

When shall I reach that happy place,
And be forever blessed?
When shall I see my Father's face,
And in his bosom rest?

Chapter 10

GRACES THAT PREPARE US FOR HEAVEN

"The soul is renewed in the glory world. The body will be fashioned after the glorious body of Jesus Christ, and both will be joined together in an indestructible bond, clearer than the indestructible moon, brighter than the sun, and more resplendent than all the heavenly spheres. For having conquered and triumphed in the church militant, the saint is now to sit down with Jesus on His throne. Hallelujah! The Lord God omnipotent reigneth. And His children shall reign with Him forever."

"An unholy man cannot enter heaven, and were he in heaven, it would be no enjoyment to him, because it is not suited to him. The nature of the resident must be suited to the place of residence. . .There is a fellowship among the devils in hell and with those who are of a diabolic nature, and we know the holy inhabitants of heaven are brethren with holy souls"—Adam Clark.

The results of Paul's argument on the resurrection of the body and its transfiguration for heaven is summarized here. "Therefore, my beloved brethren, be ye stedfast, unmoveable, always abounding in the work of the Lord, forasmuch as ye know that your labour is not in vain in the Lord" (1 Corinthians 15:58). This is to be fixed in purpose, not moved, firmly persistent, and settled to stay.

It is said of King Rehoboam,"He did evil because he set not his heart to seek the Lord" (2 Chronicles 12:14 Revised Version). "He that wavereth is like a wave of the sea driven with the wind and tossed. For let not that man think that he shall receive any thing of the Lord. A double-minded man is unstable in all his ways" (James 1:6-8). Instability loses heaven. "My heart is fixed, oh God, my heart is fixed" (Psalm 57:7). That is, his heart was settled, and immovable for heaven. *No one goes to heaven whose heart is not already there!*

Enduring To The End

Perseverance is a heaven-winning grace. The king of Israel lost his conquest because he struck the ground only three times when he should have struck twice that number. He missed by stopping. We miss heaven by not persevering. Faintheartedness, weariness, and letting go are fatal conditions in the ascent to heaven. "And let us not be weary in well doing: for in due season we shall reap, if we faint not" (Galatians 6:9). It takes strength to gain heaven. There will be much in this life to create faintheartedness and much to discourage. To hold on will require fortitude and persevering courage.

The ability to die is a heaven-gaining virtue. Paul says, "I die daily" (1 Corinthians 15:31). He wanted his dying fashioned after the perfect pattern of Christ. "Conformable unto his death" (Philippians 3:10). "I am crucified with Christ: nevertheless I live; yet not I, but Christ liveth in me: and the life which I now live in the flesh I live by the faith of the Son of God, who loved me, and gave himself for me" (Galatians 2:20). Again the apostle says, "But God forbid that I should glory, save in the cross of our Lord Jesus Christ, by whom the world is crucified unto me, and I unto the world" (Galatians 6:14).

Along the heavenly way the cross must be borne. The cross is the true sign that we are in the heavenly way. As Jesus bore the cross, so must all His true disciples do the same. As Jesus died on the cross to save from sin, so must we die to sin, to self, and to the world. It is a painful but crowning death.

As Jesus went to His Father's right hand from the cross, so we go to His right hand by way of the cross. Without the shame of the cross, there can be no joys of the crown. If there is no death of the cross, there can be no life of the crown. "It is a faithful saying: For if we be dead with him, we shall also live with him: If we suffer, we shall also reign with him: if we deny him, he also will deny us" (2 Timothy 2:11-12).

Experiencing The Divine Nature

The first chapter of second Peter lists a catalog of the heavenly-fitting graces! "And besides this, giving all diligence, add to your faith virtue; and to virtue knowledge; and to knowledge temperance; and to temperance patience; and to patience godliness; And to godliness brotherly kindness; and to brotherly kindness charity" (2 Peter 1:5-7).

The apostle has been writing of the wonderful provision that God made for our salvation. "According as his divine power hath given unto us all things that pertain unto life and godliness, through the knowledge of him that hath called us to glory and virtue: "Whereby are given unto us exceeding great and precious promises: that by these ye might be partakers of the divine nature, having escaped the corruption that is in the world through lust" (2 Peter 1:3-4).

This statement summarizes God's great design, and we must be willing to contribute our quota. In all things concerning heaven, diligence is a necessary virtue. Sustained perseverance is of vital importance. Sloth and ease ensnare every earthly action and effort, especially in the effort for heaven. To be insincere about heaven is a crime of great magnitude, eternal in fatal consequences.

He who wants to win eternal life must be deeply sincere. He must express that earnestness through laborious and persistent effort. There can be no slacking of diligence until the heavenly gates are entered. This diligence must be put forth to bring to being and perfection all the graces that prepare us for heaven.

This is not to say that you can *work* your way to heaven, for you are "saved through faith; and not of yourselves; it is the gift of God" (Ephesians 2:9). Yet, "faith without works is dead" (James 2:20). Jesus said, "If ye keep my commandment, ye shall abide in my love" (John 15:10). These scriptures clearly show that works do not *save* us but they show Jesus *where our hearts are.*

Building Blocks Of Christian Character

Faith is the foundation stone of the whole spiritual building. Faith builds on Jesus Christ. A foundation will be ruined if a house is not eventually built on it. Snow, rain, sunshine, and wind will dissolve a foundation of steel if no house is built on it. On faith's foundation, by all diligence, the spiritual superstructure must be built. The word "add" is taken from the leader of a chorus and means to bring forward and supply all things necessary to complete the chorus. Our heavenly character must be complete and harmonious.

Virtue is to be added. Virtue is a lofty endowment. It means manly vigor, made of manly qualities. Courage is a chief and distinguishing idea in virtue.

Knowledge is general understanding and intelligence. It involves the intelligent apprehension of divine truths and a thorough conviction of their importance. This knowledge is gained through reading the Bible in the light of God's Spirit. We are to seek the spirit of revelation in the knowledge of Jesus. More and more we are to "know him, and the power of his resurrection" (Philippians 3:10). Knowledge is power, strength, and light. We are to be deeply convicted of the truths of Christianity and must have a personal knowledge of what the Scriptures teach. Light and wisdom in the inner man are to be added day by day as lessons for heaven's graduating day.

Temperance follows, and this word is not limited in its meaning to intoxicants. It means self-government. We have learned about ourselves through knowledge. Self-control bears its fruit of heavenly wisdom. The tempers, passions, appetites, and desires are all held in by the strong reins of temperance. Intemperant souls cannot enter heaven. A passionless man may be in excess through his desires after money, business success, and pleasures. We must be self-governed for God and trained in the school of temperance for heaven.

Patience combines with these other graces to perfect in us the Christian character that fits us for the heavenly life. In this noble word there is always a background of manliness. With patience the Christian must contend against the various hindrances, persecutions, and temptations that conflict with his inner self and his outer world. Manliness never loses heart or courage, never charges God foolishly, and is not hasty or revengeful to man.

Godliness—God-likeness—brings the heavenly racer into a heavenly atmosphere. He is no longer simply after virtue, knowledge, temperance, and patience, which are principles, but after the pattern of a person. He is looking heavenward for a pattern that will shape his conduct and character. "Be ye holy for I am holy" (1 Peter 1:16). The struggle for heaven reaches its brightest point when man begins to struggle to be like God. Higher relationships than those on earth bind him. He is struggling for God's perfect image, that he may be a reflection of the divine Person.

He has passed into the divine family. His relationship to God gives him a new kinship to man. Love is to rule in a family circle. A brotherhood has been established in the family of God. *Brotherly love* is one of the germs of our conversion to God and one of the elements of the heavenly life. The brotherhood of earth should be like the brotherhood of heaven.

Grace keeps and polishes the natural virtues. They are burnished and refined and adorn humanity with a richness not wholly their own. But grace has features that separate it from and elevate it above all other virtues. It is original and unrivaled in its super-excellence.

The Quality Of Grace

Paul has a beautiful presentation of the practical side of piety, its most beautiful side; for in no shape is religion as lovely as when in action. Paul described grace in these words: "Be kindly affectioned one to another with brotherly love; in honour preferring one another" (Romans 12:10). This is a costly grace; like the most precious gems, it is rare, secured by great labor and cost.

Jewels such as these verses are abundantly found in God's Word. They adorn almost every page. To transfer them to our fallen and marred race is difficult. To transplant these sensitive and rare plants is a hard and delicate task. Fine spiritual graces do not seem to be the product of this hurrying age. We value bulk quantity rather than quality.

Christianity must not only present a model to the world but it must supply practical illustrations also.

"In honour preferring one another." This may be fitly termed *the crowning grace*. To put others along side of us is generous and gracious, but to put them before us is divine. To wait in order for them to catch up would be kind, but to step aside so others may pass before us in a race for honor is far above nature. To prefer others before ourselves, in heart and action, seems to bewilder our untried heads. It is too high. We sigh out in despair, "We cannot do it." But faith says, "I can do all things through Christ which strengtheneth me" (Philippians 4:13).

Crowning of others by discrowning and refusing self is grievous to flesh and blood. Yet it comes to us as a command, in the form of law. But the New Testament law unfolds the promise and supplies the help to obey. We are to put others before ourselves. This is the complete conquest of self and requires a great victory. He who has gained this is worthy to triumph through the gates into heaven!

Bearing Fruit Through Diligence

Have we learned this lesson and gained this height? Have we received the crown of this grace? Can we in honor prefer another? Has the reign of ambition ceased and the love of the world been destroyed? Has self been crucified? The death of all these must enrich the soul before it can produce this divine fruit.

It is as if God said to His people, "You, by your diligence, furnish these graces, and I will furnish heaven. You seek these spiritual graces in their abounding fullness, and I will supply to you an abounding entrance into heaven." To gain heaven hereafter, we must gain these rich graces here. Heaven grows in the soil of the God-prepared heart. We seek heaven by seeking these heavenly virtues.

Peter, concluding this earnest exhortation concerning those graces which fit us for heaven, gives us these words: "For if these things be in you, and abound, they make you that ye shall neither be barren nor unfruitful in the knowledge of our Lord Jesus Christ" (2 Peter 1:8). To fail in having these heavenly characteristics is to be blind to eternal matters and short-sighted about heaven. It is also to lose what we have already obtained. Past forgiveness amounts to nothing if we do not add to this initial step the succeeding stages, which mark the way to heaven.

"But he that lacketh these things is blind, and cannot see afar off, and hath forgotten that he was purged from his old sins" (2 Peter 1:9). Again this humble apostle calls us to diligence, with the addition of these graces as the only safeguard from backsliding and final apostasy. "Wherefore the rather, brethren, give diligence to make your calling and election sure: for if ye do these things, ye shall never fall" (2 Peter 1:10).

Then he shows the result of this diligence, toil, and the obtainment of these divine graces on heaven: "For so an entrance shall be ministered unto you abundantly into the everlasting kingdom of our Lord and Saviour Jesus Christ" (2 Peter 1:11). Or, as the Revised Version has it, "For thus shall be richly supplied unto you the entrance into the eternal kingdom of our Lord and Saviour Jesus Christ."

Let cares like a wild deluge come,
And storms of sorrow fall,

So I but safely reach my home,
My God, my heaven, my all.

There I shall bathe my weary soul
In seas of heavenly rest,
And not a wave of trouble roll
Across my peaceful breast—Isaac Watts.

Chapter 11

THE LOVE OF JESUS

"In heaven we shall live in our own element. We are now like fish in a small vessel of water, only enough to keep them alive. But what is that compared to the ocean? We have here a little air to let us breath, but what is that compared to the sweet and fresh gales upon Mount Zion? Here we have a beam of the sun to lighten our darkness and a warm ray to keep us from freezing. But there we shall live in the light and be revived by its heat"—Richard Baxter.

The apostle James says: "Blessed is the man that endureth temptation: for when he is tried, he shall receive the crown of life, which the Lord hath promised to them that love him" (James 1:12) The great condition of this reward, the crown of life, is love.

We cannot overestimate the importance of love Christ makes it the aim of the moral code and the fulfillment of all prophecy. Love fulfills the royal law and is the bond of perfection, the test of disci-

90

pleship, the first of the graces, and the shield on the day of judgment.

The thirteenth chapter of first Corinthians shows the meaning of love. We gaze at and admire these words, but rarely do we practice them. Love is not faith, but it is the only medium faith will work in. And although love is not hope, it forms the substance that hope colors and brightens. While love is the most common expression on our lips, it seldom exists in our hearts; it is easy to say but hard to do.

A Divine Portrait Of Love

What is Paul's description? Love has passion, but neither envy nor jealousy have any place in that pure flame. Clothed with humility, neither vanity nor pride inflates its heart nor speaks from its lips.

Love is never provoked to irritation nor insulted to bitterness and wrath. It does not suspect ill or avenge wrong. It is saddened by the triumph of evil but rejoices in the success of truth. Love is like God in its freedom from hasty and angry excitements and its long-suffering and self-restraint. But to Christians, love is mobile and useful.

It has strength to bear, is credulous for good, and is full of hope and cheer for the best. When faith, fortitude, and hope have almost failed, love patiently waits.

Such is the portrait of divine love. (See 1 Corinthians 13:4-8.) Such are the principles on which

Christ proposes to reconstruct human nature—sublime principles of the Son of God. He proposes to complete His building and make His heaven from the material of love.

Christianity is based on this one principle. All else is foreign or false. The commandment that completes and dominates the whole is "Love one another" (John 15:12). This is the decalog revised and completed—the Sinai of Calvery. It is the law of the gospel.

Love is the regenerating principle implanted in man's heart by the Holy Spirit. Man must labor with incessant effort and prayer for its perfection.

Our love for Jesus retires sacred attachments and becomes the crown of our earthly lives. "Where I am, there ye may be also" (John 14:3). "To be present with the Lord" (2 Corinthians 5:8). "To be with Christ; which is far better" (Philippians 1:23). "Father, I will that they also, whom thou hast given me, be with me where I am" (John 17:24).

To love Jesus is to long to be with Him. To love Jesus is to think about Him. To love Jesus is to obey Him readily and implicitly, not feebly and reluctantly. "If ye love me, keep my commandments. If ye keep my commandments, ye shall abide in my love" (John 14:15; 15:10). The certainty of heaven is assured when we keep Jesus in the center of our hearts and lives. He is to be the author of impulse, desire, effort, and action.

"Whatsoever ye do in word or deed, do all in the name of the Lord Jesus" (Colossians 3:17).

Results Of Obedience

What is Jesus to you? Does He draw you heavenward? Do you seek heaven because you want to be with Him? Is He the fairest flower in its garden? Is He the rarest and most precious of all its jewels? Is He sweeter than all of heaven's songs?

Does Jesus stir your longings for heaven? Does the desire to see and be with Him stir your soul? Jesus and heaven are bound together. To love Him with passionate devotion is heaven begun, continued, and ended. Paul says: "I am now ready to be offered, and the time of my departure is at hand. I have fought a good fight, I have finished my course, I have kept the faith: Henceforth there is laid up for me a crown of righteousness, which the Lord, the righteous judge, shall give me at that day: and not to me only, but unto all them also that love his appearing" (2 Timothy 4:6-8).

The crown is not only personal to Paul but "unto all them that love his appearing." Here it is not simply love for Jesus personally, but love for the great fact that is to culminate in His great glory. To "love his appearing" is absolutely necessary for loving His *Person*. We love the fact because we love the Person. We are not charged to love any theory about the manner or time of His coming, but the fact. Let Him come when He will, how He will, and for what purpose He will. We love His coming because we love Him. "Even so, come Lord Jesus" (Revelation 22:20).

The overcomers and conquerors are the heaven-crowned ones. Their valorous strength, undaunted courage, dire conflict, and unyielding steadfastness holds them unto death. By their Christian constancy and courage, they are kept unharmed and spotless from all the assaults of the world and are crowned to the heavenly life.

They have gained the victory over the devil. "I write unto you, young men, because ye have overcome the wicked one" (1 John 2:13). They have overcome the spirit of antichrist. "For whatsoever is born of God overcometh the world: and this is the victory that overcometh the world, even our faith. Who is he that overcometh the world, but he that believeth that Jesus is the Son of God" (1 John 5:4-5). "He that overcometh shall inherit all things; and I will be his God, and he shall be my son" (Revelation 21:7).

The saints are all robed in spotless white and bear conquering palms. (See Revelation 7:9.) They are the victors. The conflict is past, the battle has been fought, and the victory has been won forever. They are "more than conquerors through him that loved" them (Romans 8:37). Jesus has always led them in triumph, and now they are with Him upon His throne in their last and great triumph.

This love is born of the Spirit of God and is centered in Jesus Christ. Heaven depends on our

love to the Savior of sinners. We love heaven only
as we love and seek Him. This love is to be ardent
and supreme. Jesus is the joy and glory of heaven.

> *Do not I love thee, O my Lord?*
> *Then let me nothing love;*
> *Dead be my heart to every joy,*
> *When Jesus cannot move.*

> *Thou know'st I love thee, dearest Lord,*
> *But O, I long to soar*
> *Far from the sphere of mortal joys,*
> *And learn to love thee more!*

Chapter 12

LOOKING TO HEAVEN

"Salvation is the only necessary thing. This clay-idol, the world, is not to be sought. Contend for salvation. Your master, Christ, won heaven with strokes. It is a besieged castle; it must be taken with violence. Oh, this world thinks heaven is next door, and that godliness sleeps in a bed of down until it comes to heaven! But that will not do it"—Samuel Rutherford.

The Christian's attitude toward heaven must be one of desire. Paul puts it this way: "I am in a strait betwixt two, having a desire to depart, and to be with Christ; which is far better" (Philippians 1:23). To long for heaven and be with Jesus was Paul's attitude. Jesus has the very best for His disciples. God gives Jesus the key to everything, and Jesus turns everything over to His followers. This ought to kindle and inflame our desire.

We cannot move heavenward with a chilled heart or a cold purpose. "For in this we groan, earnestly desiring to be clothed upon with our house which is from heaven: If so be that being clothed we shall not be found naked" (2 Corinthians 5:2-3). It is and must be an *earnest* desire. We start toward heaven in a spark and ought to be fanned to an intense flame at each step.

The Christian's attitude toward heaven must not simply be to get rid of our cumbersome, tent-like bodies. Death has no fascination for the true Christian, but he does not fear to die or fear to live. Life has little for him apart from heaven, and death has no appeal aside from heaven.

A Glorious Future

Paul says, "For we that are in this tabernacle do groan, being burdened: not for that we would be unclothed, but clothed upon, that mortality might be swallowed up of life" (2 Corinthians 5:4). This supposes a desire so full of expectations and longings that it burdens. Heaven is so attractive, bright, and deathless under an immortal hope that present burdens become an intolerable load. Earth is a vast cemetery, and to stay is to live in the graveyard. Everything foreshadows and breathes death. The desire for heaven is kindled at the fountain of life, where we become sick of the dead and dying. Having tasted of the spring of life, the soul yearns to plunge into its immeasurable ocean.

To desire heaven is to desire life. Here, death reigns, imprisons, and ruins. There, life reigns, emancipates, and enriches. We must be patient for eternal life. Sick of death, we aspire to life by living and longing for heaven. This groaning for heaven is not natural. The Holy Spirit changes and fashions us for heaven. "Now he that hath wrought us for the selfsame thing is God, who also hath given unto us the earnest of the Spirit" (2 Corinthians 5:5).

God has fashioned us for this heavenly life. He implants in us these heavenly desires. Looking and longing for heaven are the results of God's work of grace in our hearts. He puts the Holy Spirit in us to keep heaven's memory alive and our hands busy for heaven. God works this mighty heavenly work in us so that we don't look at the things that are temporal and perishing.

These are materialized and materializing times. Materialized times always exalt the earthly and degrade the heavenly. True Christianity always diminishes the earthly and augments the heavenly. If God's watchmen are not brave, diligent, and sleepless, Christianity will catch the contagion of the times and think little of and struggle less for heaven.

Drawn Home To Heaven

God was the architect and builder of heaven's magnificence and glory. It is His dwelling place, city, and capital. It is the home of His family, and the dwelling place of His earthly elect. God fashions every child of His after the pattern of heaven and trains every soldier of His for its warfare. When the eye is dim heavenward, the luster of

God fades from the spirit, the work of God is checked in the soul, the life of God feebly pulsates, and the love of God is chilled to the heart.

"For this selfsame thing"—this heavenly fashion, these heavenly tastes, and heavenly longings—says the apostle, "is God, who also hath given unto us the earnest of the Spirit" (2 Corinthians 7:11; 5:5). Not only does this work of God shape and mold us after heaven, but the true work of God in us gives a foretaste and pledge of the heavenly.

To the true Christian, heaven is not mere sentiment, poetry, or dreamland, but it is solid in strength and home-drawing in sweetness. God is never happier with His earthly saints than when their heavenly trend is strongly marked. Heavenly longings are plainly and emphatically declared by saints whose devotion to heaven has estranged them from earth. He is not ashamed to be called their God. For them He has prepared a city.

What does God think of us who have no sighings for heaven? God's throne is in heaven. His power, person, and glory are preeminently there. Does God attract and hold us? Then heaven attracts and holds. Do we thirst after God?

Jerusalem, my happy home!
Name ever dear to me!
When shall my labors have an end,
In joy and peace, and thee?

When shall these eyes thy heaven-built walls
And pearly gates behold?
Thy bulwarks with salvation strong,
And streets of shining gold?

O when, thou city of my God,
Shall I thy courts ascend,
Where congregations ne'er break up,
And sabbaths have no end?

Chapter 13

RACING DOWN THE STRETCH

"God will manage our affairs if we are filled with His affairs. Be sure you are in God's hands and not that of an ecclesiasticism. I am very feeble. I want to live for God and to depart and be with Christ. I have an unspeakable desire to know the future, to see it and enjoy it, and to be there to see and enjoy. Let us hold on to God"— E.M. Bounds.

The Christian is on a stretch for heaven. With all his power taxed and strained in a movement, he is in a race for heaven. "Know ye not that they which run in a race run all, but one receiveth the prize? So run, that ye may obtain. And every man that striveth for the mastery is temperate in all things. Now they do it to obtain a corruptible crown; but we an incorruptible. I therefore so run, not as uncertainly; so fight I, not as one that beateth the air: But I keep under my body, and bring it into subjection: lest that by any means, when I have preached to others, I myself should be a castaway" (1 Corinthians 9:24-27).

Here we have the picture of the heavenly athlete putting forth all his strength to win the prize of an incorruptible crown. The Greek athlete, in his exertion to win the corruptible crown, is a favorite Bible illustration that stirs men for heaven. The athlete has no eye except for the crown. Every particle of his strength is put under strain to secure that end, and we are charged to "so run that we may obtain."

Jesus impresses the same idea on the multitude in reply to the question: "Then said one unto him, Lord, are there few that be saved? And he said unto them, Strive to enter in at the straight gate: for many, I say unto you, will seek to enter in, and shall not be able" (Luke 13:23-24). *Strive* means *to agonize* with intense effort.

Running To Win

Hebrews declares that heaven is gained only by the most intense and persistent effort. Former winners are represented as having gained the prize and have arranged themselves as spectators of the renowned and exciting conflict. Jesus Christ, having passed over and marked the way, is seated at the goal to judge the race and award the crown. The racers are charged most solemnly, "Wherefore, seeing we also are compassed about with so great a cloud of witnesses, let us lay aside every weight, and the sin which doth so easily beset us, and let us run with patience the race that is set before us, looking unto Jesus the author and finisher of our faith; who for the joy that was set before him endured the cross, despising the shame, and is set down at the right hand of the throne of God" (Hebrews 12:1-2).

Where in all the pages of literature could there be a stronger call to throw all energy and weight into the conflict? The issue centers on the racer and his ability to run, outstrip, and lay aside all things which embarrass or impede progress. An incorruptible crown is the reward. Immortality and eternal life hang on the issue.

Paul charges Timothy to be on the same stretch for heaven. People will not be on the stretch for heaven if their preachers are not. Paul desires Timothy to lay himself out in the race to "fight the good fight of faith" (1 Timothy 6:12). The word "fight" means intense effort and agony. Paul had been writing to Timothy about the love of money and its pernicious and damning results. Then he charges him to flee as a man of God from these things. As worldly men agonize with desire and toil after money, Timothy, as a man of God, was to agonize and labor for heaven and its imperishable riches.

Pressing Toward The Mark

Paul gives a vivid view of a stretch for heaven: "That I may know him, and the power of his resurrection, and the fellowship of his sufferings, being made conformable unto his death; If by any means I might attain unto the resurrection of the dead. Not as though I had already attained, either were already perfect: but I follow after, if that I may apprehend that for which also I am apprehended for Christ Jesus. Brethren, I count not myself to have apprehended: but this one thing I do, forgetting those things which are behind, and reaching forth unto those things which are before, I press toward the mark for the prize of the high calling of God in Christ Jesus. Let us, therefore, as many as be perfect, be thus minded: and if in anything ye be otherwise minded, God shall reveal even this unto you" (Philippians 3:10-15).

Paul purposed to win heaven, not by his marvelous conversion or his high apostolate, but by striving after heaven all his life. He was on a stretch for heaven. With all the energy of his imperial nature, ardor, and intensity, he could forget "those things which are behind" in the eagerness and strength of pressing forward. "Reaching forth to those that are before," means stretching forward in eagerness, energy, and intentiveness of pursuit. "I press toward the mark" is the figure of running with swiftness and energy. All this shows a perseverance to hold the whole being in the fullest concentration of strength to gain the end.

Paul could not afford to miss heaven. But even an apostle can only make sure of heaven by being on the stretch *always* and *everywhere*. May this example stir us to the most profound depths.

"Brethren, be followers together of me, and mark them which walk so as ye have us for an ensample" (Philippians 3:17).

> Racers of Christ, arise,
> Stand forth, prepare to run:
> Toward the goal lift up your eyes,
> And manfully go on.
>
> 'Tis true the race is short,
> But then it is not long;
> Each racer soon will take his harp,
> And warble Zion's song.

Chapter 14

TO KNOW IS TO LOVE

"Fasten your grips on Christ. Let not this clay portion of earth take up your soul. You are a child of God. Therefore, seek your Father's heritage. Send up your heart to see the dwelling house and fair rooms in the New City. Shame upon those who cry, 'Up with the world, and down with conscience and heaven!'"—Samuel Rutherford.

The Christian's attitude to heaven is one of *knowledge*. "For we *know* that, if our earthly house of this tabernacle were dissolved, we have a building of God, a house not made with hands, eternal in the heavens" (2 Corinthians 5:1).

The Christian stands certain of death as all the living do. His body is a frail tent and an heir of death hastening to decay. But the Christian knows that "if this earthly house were dissolved, he has a house not made with hands eternal in the heavens."

His knowledge about heaven is not a mere wish

or hope. God has committed Himself in the strongest way to give knowledge and assurance of heaven to all His children. The Spirit Himself bears witness to our adoption and heirship. (See 1 John 5:6.)

Sealed By The Spirit

In regard to this great fact of our names being written in the Book of Life, we are not left in ignorance. God seals us with the Holy Spirit that is the promise as well as a witness. A witness bears testimony. He has heaven in conscious realization, though perhaps not in full measure. The true Christian is no agnostic. He knows some things.

Heaven, in this life, is not as large a reality to him as it will be when his feet are on the city's gold pavement. His faith brings to him the very substance of things hoped for, and his hope makes the present luminous and strong. Christian faith and hope make the things of heaven real, conscious, and tangible. The knowledge of his home in heaven defies death, change, and misfortune! How attractive that "building of God, eternal in the heavens" (2 Corinthians 5:1).

Can we be certain about our home on high? Is there a blessed surety?

Yes, we know. The Word of God tells us. The Spirit of God has spoken it to our hearts and left its sweetness there. "And we desire that every one of you do shew the same diligence to the full assurance of hope unto the end: That ye be not slothful, but followers of them who through faith and patience inherit the promises" (Hebrews 6:11-12).

We have been examining our heavenly title deeds lately, and they are signed and sealed. The house is built, the lot is numbered, and "we *know* that, if our earthly house of this tabernacle were dissolved, we have a building of God, a house not made with hands, eternal in the heavens."

Death makes no pauper of the Christian. It only brings him to his inheritance. Death is the best thing that can come to the Christian because it puts him in possession of his great fortune and brings him to his home. We should go through life with radiance and triumph. We, like the saints of old, ought to take joyfully the spoiling of our possessions, knowing in ourselves that in heaven we have a better and enduring substance. (See Hebrews 10:34.)

Thine earthly Sabbaths, Lord, we love;
But there's a nobler rest above:
To that our lab'ring souls aspire,
With ardent pangs of strong desire.

No more fatigue, no more distress;
Nor sin nor hell shall reach the place;
No sighs shall mingle with the songs
Which warble from immortal tongues.

No rude alarms of raging foes;

No cares to break the long repose;
No midnignt shade, no clouded sun,
But sacred, high, eternal noon.

O long-expected day, begin;
Dawn on these realms of woe and sin:
Fain would we leave this weary road,
And sleep in death, to rest with God.

Chapter 15

CITIZENS OF THE KINGDOM

"Love heaven. Let your heart be in it. Up, up and visit the new land and view the fair city, the white throne, and the Lamb—run fast, for it is late"—Samuel Rutherford.

The Bible puts our citizenship in heaven by such a naturalization force that we are alienated from earth. The sighings of an exile for his native land, and the weariness, longings, and loneliness of pilgrims are typical responses of the true Christian. The Bible puts them in the attitude of groaning after and living for heaven. To them the only life is to live for and in heaven.

The term heaven signifies a place of exaltation and glory. It is God's dwelling place. It is the land of a higher order of beings and things than exist on earth.

It is called "the third heaven" from its loftiness and supremacy, in contrast with the lower heavens. (See 2 Corinthians 12:2.) The good man is to lay up his treasures in heaven and constantly fix his heart and eye there. Heaven is where Jesus has gone and is preparing a place for us. Heaven is a land very dear to the Christian's heart. The heart beats quicker and the eye grows brighter at the mention of it!

Our Father dwells there. Jesus came from heaven on His great mission. The Holy Spirit came down from heaven. The bodies of Enoch, Elijah, and Christ are there. Perhaps the bodies of the saints who came out of their graves when Jesus was raised from the dead are in heaven. The spirits of all the holy dead are there. An innumerable company are there, safe, blessed, tearless, and immortal.

The Comfort Of Home

Heaven ought to draw on our hearts and lift us above earth! It should fill our thoughts and brighten our hopes! Heaven ought to ease our griefs, banish our fears, lift care from our hearts, and make us immune to the ills of this life. Jesus lifted His eye and heart to heaven in order to endure the cross and despise the shame. (See Hebrews 12:2.) We also ought to fix our eyes on heaven. It should be the aim of our lives, the goal of our ambition, and the stimulant of every exertion. Our names should be written there, and our treasures laid up there.

Heaven is our native land, fatherland, and home.

"For our conversation is in heaven; from

whence also we look for the Saviour, the Lord Jesus Christ" (Philippians 3:20).

The Revised Version changes the word "conversation" to "citizenship," and in the margin it has "commonwealth." The word has to do with a state and its laws, regulations, and citizens.

"To day," said Jesus to the dying thief, "shalt thou be with me in paradise" (Luke 23:43). Paul said he "was caught up into paradise," another name for Eden, the abode of our first parents (2 Corinthians 12:4). The name is transferred to the abode of the saints in heaven and is called the "paradise of God" (Revelation 2:7). The first paradise was made for man, with every tree that is pleasant to the sight and good for food. Beauty, purity, and innocence were there. The second paradise will contain all these in greater proportion.

In the first paradise: "The Lord God planted a garden" (Genesis 2:8). In the second paradise: "He hath prepared for them a city" (Hebrews 11:16). The contrast and advance are from a garden to a city. The first was *man's paradise*. The second, the "paradise of God." Man was in the first paradise. God is in the second paradise. God *visited* the first paradise, but He *dwells* in the second paradise!

Heaven involves the common well-being and happiness of the whole people, not of any favored class. Heaven's government is perfect, and happiness is everyone's privilege.

We have the idea of heaven as a place: "heaven;

from whence also we look for the Saviour" (Philippians 3:20). Jesus must occupy a place, and that place must be heaven. We look for Him to come from heaven and do His work of raising the dead and changing the bodies of His saints.

"Who shall change our vile body, that it may be fashioned like unto his glorious body, according to the working whereby he is able even to subdue all things unto himself" (Philippians 3:21).

The Christian has his citizenship in heaven. His allegiance is to God and his loyalty to heaven. He is bound to obey the laws of heaven. *The best citizen of heaven is the best citizen of earth.* He is bound by highest obligations to obedience, virtue, and government. How exalted are citizens of such a divine commonwealth!

In the days of Rome's power, "I am a Roman," carried with it dignity, honor, and safety. "I am a citizen of heaven" ought to represent dignity, nobility, purity, and heavenliness!

O Paradise! O Paradise!
I want to sin no more,
I want to be as pure on earth
As on thy spotless shore;

O Paradise! O Paradise!
I greatly long to see
The special place my dearest Lord
In love prepares for me;

Lord Jesus, King of Paradise,
O keep me in thy love,
And guide me to that happy land
Of perfect rest above.

Chapter 16

A PILGRIM'S JOURNEY HOME

"Heaven is called a kingdom for its immense greatness, and a city because of its great beauty and population. It is full of inhabitants of all nations, many angels, and an infinite number of the just, even as many as have died since the death of Abel. And there shall repair all such as will die in Christ to the end of the world; and after the general judgment will there remain forever invested in their glorious bodies. How happy it will be to live with such persons"—
Jeremy Taylor.

Hebrews, speaking of Old Testament saints, says, "These all died in faith, not having received the promises, but having seen them afar off, and were persuaded of them, and embraced them, and confessed that they were strangers and pilgrims on the earth. For they that say such things declare plainly that they seek a country" (Hebrews 11:13-14). The Revised Version changes this so that it reads: "For they that say such things make it manifest that they are seeking after a country of their own."

The English word "country" does not give the idea strong enough. The word is defined: one's native country, fatherland, and own country. Heaven is our home and fatherland. Here, we are foreigners, pilgrims, and strangers. The loneliness and longing of a stranger and weariness of a pilgrim should be ours. The heart-sighing and exiled yearnings should declare to all that we are not at home. We are not native to these skies, but heaven-born, seeking the heavenly country.

A Pilgrim's Desire And Duty

Heaven ought to draw and engage us. Heaven ought to so fill our hearts and characters that all would see that we are strangers to this world, natives of a land fairer than this. We must be out of tune with this world. The very atmosphere of earth should be chilling to us, and its companionship dull and insipid. Heaven is our native home, and death to us is birth. Heaven should kindle desire and, like a magnet, draw us upward to the skies. Duty to God, alone, should hold us here.

Paul was torn between desire and duty. Christ and heaven had his heart, but duty kept him in exile. "For me to live is Christ, and to die is gain. But if I live in the flesh, this is the fruit of my labor: yet what I shall choose I wot not. For I am in a strait betwixt two, having a desire to depart, and to be with Christ; which is far better: Nevertheless to abide in the flesh is more needful for you. And having this confidence, I know that I shall abide and continue with you all for your furtherance and joy of faith" (Philippians 1:21-25).

Those ancient believers spoken of in Hebrews 11 discovered that they were all pilgrims and strangers on the earth with heavenly longings. For the hearts that are settled here, heaven is a strange, far-off land! These ancient pilgrims transferred their homeland to the heavenly country. God noted their fidelity and heard their sighing. He was not ashamed of them and built a city for them.

In writing to the Corinthians about the Christian's attitude toward heaven, Paul said in the Revised Version, "We are willing rather to be absent from the body and to be at home with the Lord" (2 Corinthians 5:8). Here we have one of the strongest, sweetest, and most attractive symbols of heaven. Home—sacred, dear, restful, delightful, and full of holy feelings and deathless ties. In heaven, these will be ten thousand times stronger and sweeter.

Homesick For Heaven

At home in heaven! What satisfaction! What rest to tired feet and hearts! What a sense of security and confidence! Earth's green, glad soil can never produce the home feeling as profound, satisfying, and restful as in heaven. Not only will we realize it as home when we get there, but all along the way

117

heaven will draw and bind us to our heavenly world. This longing for heaven alienates us from earth and makes us homesick at heart.

With deep spiritual insight and sound spiritual philosophy, one of Scotland's most gifted and saintly preachers said, after visiting a beautiful manse, "The parsonage is altogether too sweet. Other men could hardly live there without saying, 'This is my rest.' I don't think minister's manses should ever be so beautiful."

We must constantly guard ourselves against this great peril. Earthly attachments lessen our heavenly attachments. If our hearts indulge themselves in great earthly loves, we will cheat heaven. God's great work (and often His most afflictive and chastening work) is to unfasten our hearts from earth and fasten them to heaven. He must destroy our infatuation with our earthly homes so that we seek a home in heaven.

My heavenly home is bright and fair:
No pain or death can enter there;
Its glittering towers the sun outshine;
That heavenly mansion shall be mine.

Let others seek a home below,
Which flames devour, or waves o'erflow,
Be mine the happier lot to own
A heavenly mansion near the throne
—William Hunter.

Chapter 17

TRIUMPH THROUGH TRIBULATION

"There is required patience on our part till the summer fruit of heaven be ripe for us. It is in the bud; but there are many things to do before our harvest comes. And we can hardly endure to set our paper-face to one of Christ's storms, and to go to heaven with wet feet. . . .We love to carry a heaven to heaven with us and would have two summers in one year, and no less than two heavens. But this will not do for us; one (and such a one!) may suffice us well enough. Christ has but one, and will we have two?"—Samuel Rutherford.

The hatred and persecution cast upon followers of God pierces many a saintly heart and makes them men of "sorrows and acquainted with grief" (Isaiah 53:3). They are shut out. Heavenly faith is cast out by "religion." No persecutors are so heartless and relentless as religious persecutors. No hatred is as bitter as the world's hatred.

"If the world hate you, ye know that it hated me

before it hated you. If ye were of the world, the world would love his own: but because ye are not of the world, but I have chosen you out of the world, therefore the world hateth you. Remember the word that I said unto you, The servant is not greater than his lord. If they have persecuted me, they will also persecute you" (John 15:18-20).

But from wherever and whomever these persecutions come, they are to purify and mature us. By them God's people are purged and perfected. We are not to be impatient under them! We are not to fight against or murmur at them, but endure them with sweetness and joy. James says: "My brethren, count it all joy when ye fall into divers temptations; knowing this, that the trying of your faith worketh patience. But let patience have her perfect work, that ye may be perfect and entire, wanting nothing" (James 1:2-4). This is the process.

Paul brings to our minds the same view of trials. Putting Jesus Christ in the forefront gives us fuller access to Him and a firmer standing in Him. It brings heaven into full view, with the presence of Christ and the glory of God shining through the door of undying hope!

"And not only so, but we glory in tribulations also: knowing that tribulation worketh patience; And patience, experience; and experience, hope" (Romans 5:3-4).

Joy In Tribulation

Tribulation enlarges every holy principle, precious result, and fragrant sentiment. Through tribulation patience is made more patient, enriched in sweetness and strength. Hope is enlarged in scope and vision, and its foundations are laid in jeweled adornment. "We glory in tribulations." Do we? Can we? Heaven in eye and heart enables us to do this strange work. Tribulations not only burnish and garnish our heavenly home, but add many rooms to its size and many gems to its value.

Peter leaves his thankless service of stirring up "pure minds by the way of remembrance" (2 Peter 3:1) and rises to vision, beatitude, and anthem: "Blessed be the God and Father of our Lord Jesus Christ, which according to his abundant mercy hath begotten us again unto a lively hope by the resurrection of Jesus Christ from the dead, To an inheritance incorruptible, and undefiled, and that fadeth not away, reserved in heaven for you, Who are kept by the power of God through faith unto salvation ready to be revealed in the last time. Wherein ye greatly rejoice, though now for a season, if need be, ye are in heaviness through manifold temptations: That the trial of your faith, being much more precious than of gold that perisheth, though it be tried with fire, might be found unto praise and honor and glory at the appearing of Jesus Christ: Whom having not seen ye love; in whom, though now ye see him not, yet believing, ye rejoice with joy unspeakable and full of glory" (1 Peter 1:3-8).

Here they all are—God the Father, Jesus and His

resurrection, the Spirit and sanctification, hope, heaven, love, and fiery trials. Trials clarify, refine, swell the anthems to praise, and bring heaven into a clearer and nearer vision.

"Counting it all joy" is not simply resignation. A cardinal virtue and crowning grace, tribulation is scarcely recognized as a grace at all in times of robust faith. It is not the grace of folded arms and silent hearts, but it is "Count it all joy." It is "Glory in tribulations also." Glory in tribulation as you glory in heaven, for they are one. Rejoice greatly! Rejoice with "joy unspeakable and full of glory." Rejoice in the prospect of heaven.

Glory in infirmities. Says Paul: "Therefore I take pleasure in infirmities, in reproaches, in necessities, in persecutions, in distress for Christ's sake: for when I am weak, then I am strong" (2 Corinthians 12:10).

The Beatitudes are born here, enlarged to their greatest measure and most heavenly joy. "Blessed are they which are persecuted for righteousness' sake: for theirs is the kingdom of heaven. Blessed are ye, when men shall revile you, and persecute you, and shall say all manner of evil against you falsely, for my sake. Rejoice, and be exceeding glad: for great is your reward in heaven: for so persecuted they the prophets which were before you" (Matthew 5:10-12). Christ puts these words among His diamond utterances.

The Eternal Weight Of Glory

Listen to Paul again: "For which cause we faint not; but though our outward man perish, yet the inward man is renewed day by day. For our light affliction, which is but for a moment, worketh for us a far more exceeding and eternal weight of glory; while we look not at the things which are seen, but at the things which are not seen: for the things which are seen are temporal; but the things which are not seen are eternal" (2 Corinthians 4:16-18).

Paul discredits and eases the pang of every pain and persecution! "Light affliction"—light in weight and short in time. Affliction is light compared with "the weight of glory" and short compared with eternity. Highly prized and invaluable are these afflictions as they "work for us as a far more exceeding and eternal weight of glory." Add this estimate to Christ's words, "Rejoice and be exceeding glad: for great is your reward in heaven."

But these trials work this eternal greatness of reward only if "we look not at the things which are seen but at the things which are unseen." Our eyes are taken off the things of earth and placed on the things of heaven.

Our reward is sure. The "far more exceeding and eternal weight of glory" is ours. When eyes are on the earth, trials wear into our heart's core and cause us to lose the good which they bring.

Paul judges between the suffering of this life and the glory of the future life. "For I reckon that the sufferings of this present time are not worthy to be compared with the glory which shall be revealed in us" (Romans 8:18).

Peter couples the two thoughts, suffering and heaven, into a common principle. "Beloved, think it not strange concerning the fiery trial which is to try you. As though some strange thing happened unto you: But rejoice, inasmuch as ye are partakers of Christ's sufferings; that, when his glory shall be revealed, ye may be glad also with exceeding joy. If ye be reproached for the name of Christ, happy are ye; for the Spirit of glory and of God resteth upon you: on their part he is evil spoken of, but on your part he is glorified" (1 Peter 4:12-14).

Again Peter, speaking of the devil, declares the universality of affliction wherever saints are found: "Be sober, be vigilant; because your adversary the devil, as a roaring lion, walketh about, seeking whom he may devour: Whom resist stedfast in the faith, knowing that the same afflictions are accomplished in your brethren that are in the world. But the God of all grace, who hath called us unto his eternal glory by Christ Jesus, after that ye have suffered a while, make you perfect, stablish, strengthen, settle you" (1 Peter 5:8-10).

The Chastening Process

Heaven is declared to be God's *eternal glory*. These are words far beyond dictionaries. The glory of earth's greatest one would stir the mightiest ambition and gratify the loftiest aspiration. But what measure is equal to God's eternal glory? What words can define it? And yet to that we are called—to God's "eternal glory"! But it is not to be revealed until we have suffered a while! And suffering is short in length and limited in pain when contrasted with God's eternal glory.

This chastening process often comes through persecutions from the hands of evil men and devils, yet God holds the outcome in His own hands. Nothing is outside of His power or excluded from His control. Whether they are things from the devil, evil men, or the mistakes of good men, "we know that *all things* work together for good to them that love God, to them who are the called according to his purpose" (Romans 8:28). Persecution and affliction cannot hinder God from pressing His faithful elect ones on until they are glorified.

"All that will live godly in Christ Jesus shall suffer persecution" (2 Timothy 3:12). "In the world ye shall have tribulation" (John 16:33). "If we be dead with him, we shall also live with him: If we suffer, we shall also reign with him" (2 Timothy 2:11-12). These are principles of the Christian life. There is no persecuting Roman power now, either pagan or papal. Those fierce and cruel days are gone, but there are petty persecutions. The world still hates Christ's saints, and a worldly church still rejects and bans God's own people.

Dr. Adoniram Judson writes from Burmah to a friend in America: "Remember, I pray you, that word of pioneer missionary David Brainerd. Do not think it enough to live at the rate of common Christians. True, they will call you uncharitable and critical, but what is the opinion of poor worms of the dust that it should deter us from our duty? Brainerd also said, 'Time is but a moment, life a vapor, and all its enjoyments but empty bubbles and fleeting blasts of wind.' " Again Dr. Judson writes, "Let me beg of you not to rest contented with the commonplace religion that is now prevalent."

Yet it is this rising above commonplace religion that gives offense and that awakens painful persecution. No person seeks heaven in an honest, successful way that does not rise above the average piety.

The apostle Paul charges Timothy to "follow after righteousness, godliness, faith, love, patience, meekness. Fight the good fight of faith, lay hold of eternal life" (1 Timothy 6:11-12). "Following after" these things and "laying hold of eternal life" is vital. Heaven is won by winning the heavenly virtues. Ardent pursuit after the heavenly graces is the only way to pursue heaven with fire and gain the prize. To mature and perfect these graces is to be made ready for heaven.

126

Principles Of Patience

Patience is one of those fundamental Christian virtues in which we are schooled for the heavenly life. Paul, writing to the church at Rome, says "To them who by patient continuance in well doing seek for glory and honor and immortality, eternal life" (Romans 2:7). Again he says: "In your patience possess ye your souls" (Luke 21:19). Patience is defined as the grace of endurance, literally, "staying or remaining behind." He is patient who is unmoved from his purpose and his loyalty to faith and piety by even the greatest trials.

Patience is a cardinal virtue in Christian character. It is strong and sweet, the pillar of strength. It does not succumb under sufferings. It is self-restrained and does not retaliate wrongs. Patience is brave opposed to cowardice or despondency and has nothing in common with wrath and revenge. It expresses its sweetness through every bruised and bleeding pore. It is "the kingdom and patience of our Lord Jesus Christ" (Revelation 1:9).

Patience is born and perfected in trial. "We glory," says Paul, "in tribulations also, knowing that tribulation worketh patience" (Romans 5:3). James makes this remarkable demand and statement: "Count it all joy when ye fall into divers temptations; Knowing this, that the trying of your faith worketh patience. But let patience have her perfect work, that ye may be perfect and entire, wanting nothing" (James 1:2-4). Count every trial with joy, not resignation simply, but joy. Count trials as joy at their coming and joy at their results. Trials bring perfection, maturity, and fullness. God makes our fruit perfect by perfecting our character, and character is perfected by trial.

There is no doubt about the necessity of patience to win heaven. "For ye have need of patience, that, after ye have done the will of God, ye might receive the promise" (Hebrews 10:36). "Let us run with patience the race that is set before us" (Hebrews 12:1). Job is a perfect illustration of patience because he held on to God without a shadow of turning through his manifold trials. "The Lord gave, and the Lord hath taken away; blessed be the name of the Lord" (Job 1:21) is the language of patience in its undisturbed, uncomplaining serenity and sweetness. "Though he slay me, yet will I trust in him" (Job 13:15) is the language of patience in its endurance and perseverance.

Impatience is the epidemic sin. Strong people, weak people, sick people, well people, old people, and young people—all are impatient. And all people try our patience. So how appropriate the universal injunction, "Be patient toward all men" (1 Thessalonians 5:14).

Patience is necessary to fruit-bearing. They who are ready to be reaped for the heavenly harvest, "having heard the word, keep it and bring forth fruit with patience" (Luke 8:15). This grace seems to be slow and indolent. But though Christian patience is very quiet and often silent, it is never lazy. It is "not slothful, but followers of them who through faith and patience inherit the promises" (Hebrews 6:12). Heaven is for the patient spirit. Heaven is already possessed by the patient. Has patience possessed us?

Who suffer with our Master here,
We shall before his face appear
and by his side sit down;
To patient faith the prize is sure,
And all that to the end endure
The cross, shall wear the crown.

Thrice blessed, bliss-inspiring hope!
It lifts the fainting spirits up,
It brings to life the dead:
Our conflicts here shall soon be past,
And you and I ascend at last,
Triumphant with our head—Charles Wesley.

Chapter 18

THE HOPE OF HEAVEN

*What was the earthly paradise in Eden com-
pared to that purchased by the second Adam,
who is the Lord from heaven? The price it cost
the purchaser every one knows. Having purchased it, He has gone to prepare it, to set it in
order, and lay out His skill upon it. O what a
place will Jesus make it—yes, has already made
heaven. The very place should attract us"*—NEV-
INS.

It is not the bare fact of heaven that we are
dealing with now, but the Christian grace of
heaven, which is hope. Belief is sterile and
deludes if the fact is not fashioned into a principle. If the cold facts of gospel history do not
become the fertilizers of the sweet graces of the
Spirit, then they are dead and deadening. Jesus
does not save us until the facts of the gospel enter
into our experience and become the blood of our
spiritual life.

The fact of heaven must be believed. Heaven

exists all glorious and enduring, but it must enter our experience; and then from this experience, hope is born.

Hope is a mighty spiritual principle. So strong is it that the apostle centers all the forces of salvation on it. "We are saved," he says, "by hope" (Romans 8:24). By it there comes into play all the energetic forces that save. These forces are limp and without hope. Heaven nourishes all the principles of a deep, conscious piety. It gives to hope its ripeness, richness, and power. Only the saint who strives to be like Jesus, with all the passion and brightness of hope, is truly saved. Doubt and fear flee away from such a salvation.

Living Hope

By its characteristics heavenly hope is distinguished from all false hopes that perish. Hope can lose none of its brightness. It can wait with serenity and sweetness and without murmuring. "The patience of hope" (1 Thessalonians 1:3) adds to hope's luster and sweetness. "But if we hope for that we see not, then do we with patience wait for it" (Romans 8:25).

It is termed a *good* hope, joined to everlasting consolation. What can be better than a hope that brings in everlasting consolation, a source of unfailing joy? It is also termed a *lively* or *living hope*. (See 1 Peter 1:3.) Peter is telling how this true hope came out of the grave of their dead hopes, vitalized and immortalized by the resurrec-

131

tion of Jesus Christ "to an inheritance incorruptible, and undefiled, and that fadeth not away" (1 Peter 1:4). Our hope has the imperishable life of Jesus Christ in it. It is a blessed and happy hope! It makes us happy and secure.

True Christian hope is only seen by the heart's eye. The Revised Version has it, "The eye of your heart enlightened that ye may know what is the hope of your calling" (Ephesians 1:18). Our natural eye and earthly lights do not show us "the calling," neither have they vision for "the riches of the glory of that inheritance" on which hope feeds and lives.

Hope, while it flourishes by the afflictions of life, is formed of the gentlest and mildest graces. Combining meekness with fear, hope is neither arrogant, rude, nor self-assertive but is mild, retiring, and reverential. It is a very patient grace. It perseveres and is strong to wait until its fruition comes. Hope saves from discontent, depression, and weakness.

Hope is one of the three great elements of Christian character. It is united with faith and love to give perfection, establish Christian reputation, and awaken thankfulness.

United With Faith And Love

"We give thanks to God always for you all, making mention of you in our prayers; Remembering without ceasing your work of faith, and labor of love and patience of hope in our Lord Jesus Christ, in the sight of God and our Father" (1 Thessalonians 1:2-3).

While faith exhibits itself in active works, love shows itself in exhaustive toil; hope brightens and bears all, declaring her sisterhood to the other graces by patient waiting. Hope's bright endurance mightily sustains faith, and love gives to them unfaltering and unfainting courage. They are inseparably united in the Christian life.

"And now abideth faith, hope, charity, these three; but the greatest of these is charity" (1 Corinthians 13:13).

Faith appropriates the grace of God in salvation. Love is the animating spirit of our Christian life, while hope takes hold of the future as belonging to the Lord and His own. The Kingdom of God, past, present, and future is reflected in faith, love, and hope.

How thoroughly hope impregnates the gospel system! It is essential to Christian character! How necessary hope is to Christian struggles will be seen in the many references to it in the New Testament.

"Paul, an apostle of Jesus Christ by the commandment of God our Saviour, and Lord Jesus Christ, which is our hope" (1 Timothy 1:1).

In this passage hope centers itself in our Lord Jesus Christ. He is our hope. We hang *on* Him and center all *in* Him.

This hope of a glorious Christ and heaven is not

a product of man's nature or despair or the outgrowth of his cheerful spirit but a spiritual gift.

"Now the God of hope fill you with all joy and peace in believing, that ye may abound in hope, through the power of the Holy Ghost" (Romans 15:13).

Hope has its spring and being in God. Founded on faith in God, it floods the soul with joy and peace. It increases by the presence of the Holy Spirit working in us. Hope abounds more and more as we are filled with all the fullness of God. The whole plan of salvation, its mystery and its richest glory, is summarized by Paul: "Christ in you, the hope of glory" (Colossians 1:27). Where Christ is, there hope springs to its fullness. All is barrenness, death, and despair outside of Christ.

The hope of heaven is not a mere emotion. It is not fleeting but ever enduring and strong. It burns with a steady, brilliant light. It is not a mere incident of the religious life but fundamental and organic. It goes into the being of vital godliness as an essential principle. It dwells in the Holy of Holies and is the high priest of the inner sanctuary of the soul. It sanctifies the Lord God and dwells where He dwells.

"But sanctify the Lord God in your hearts: and be ready always to give an answer to every man that asketh you a reason of the hope that is in you with meekness and fear" (1 Peter 3:15).

In hope of that immortal crown

I now the cross sustain,
And gladly wander up and down,
And smile at toil and pain:
I suffer out my threescore years,
Till my Deliverer come,
And wipe away His servant's tears,
And take His exile home—Charles Wesley.

REUNION IN HEAVEN

Strike your tent, O pilgrim,
Gird your loins and follow on;
Soon your journey's ended,
'Twill bring thee to thy God—Claud L. Chilton.

Deep and positive joy springs from the reunion of the broken and wasted loves and friendships of earth. We will see our friends and associate with them in stronger ties because we have been partners in the tears and toils of earth. The society of heaven stands out in an intense manner. Its crowds and multitudes express association; and doubtless, while there will be no selfish and exclusive circles, there will be narrow, closer, select ones within the larger.

Paul checks our sorrows for the dead with these words: "But I would not have you to be ignorant, brethren, concerning them which are asleep, that ye sorrow not, even as others which have no hope. For if we believe that Jesus died and rose again, even so them also which sleep in Jesus will God bring with him. For the Lord himself shall descend from heaven with a shout, with the voice of the archangel, and with the trump of God: and the dead in Christ shall rise first: Then we which are alive and remain shall be caught up together with them in the clouds, to meet the Lord in the air: and so shall we ever be with the Lord. Wherefore comfort one another with these words" (1 Thessalonians 4:13-14; 16-18).

We must not weep in despair over the graves of our loved ones who have left us. We have hope of meeting them again; and with them, to meet the Lord and be forever with Him and them. "Wherefore comfort one another with these words." We will see them and know them again. These are the points of divine comfort in the apostle's words. Even here on earth this comfort makes us victors over death, takes its sting away, wipes the tears from our eyes, and wreathes our hearts with fadeless hopes.

Gathering Before The Throne

Many are the attractions of heaven, all of which should win us from the vain and dying things of earth. First of all, Jesus, our great High Priest, is there. He is the sun and center of the heavenly world. Then many things that make earth undesirable—sickness, sorrow, pain, and death—will be absent. Added to all these glorious things that should draw us like a strong magnet to heaven is the blessed hope of a glorious reunion with loved ones who have gone on before.

Not only does Paul give us an indication of this pleasing prospect, but John shows us the things he saw when "a door was opened in heaven" (Revelation 4:1). He tells us who are in heaven—God, Jesus Christ, the Lamb of God, the angels, and those who "have washed their robes and made them white in the blood of the Lamb" (Revelation 7:14).

Who are among these last named? Look back over life and imagine the faces of friends once loved, who broke away from us, disappeared from view, and now are "before the throne of God" (Revelation 7:15). Some of these were of our own households. Some whose vacant chairs are but sad reminders of them, "absent from the body, but now present with the Lord."

Where are they? "Before the throne" in God's presence in intimate association with their Redeemer. They are in heaven itself, where "they serve him day and night" (Revelation 7:15). Their faces peer at us over the walls of the celestial city, their eyes look at us in imagination as we gaze heavenward, and their hands beckon to us in our heavenward journey.

Will we ever see them again? Yes, if our robes are washed in the blood of the Lamb and if we are faithful in tribulation.

Will we know them in that land of light, liberty, and fullness of joy? By all means! For if Moses and

Elijah were recognized on the mount of transfiguration—if Stephen knew his Lord as they were stoning him—if the rich man in hell recognized Lazarus and Abraham though far off in heaven—then there is no doubt that we will know one another in that land. We will not lose our identity in heaven and will have the same peculiarities and specific make-up in our entire moral being. In heaven there is no death, sorrow, crying, pain, or separations, "for the former things are passed away" (Revelation 21:4).

Oh, the blessed hope of a glad reunion with departed saints in the glory world! How they attract us when we look that way!

What a vision of glory! What ecstasy came to the apostle Paul, this saintly man, from his association with Jesus Christ! Almost unnumbered are the illustrations of a truth so resonant of grace that Jesus, even in this life, is the greatest treasure, the most profound joy, and the most gracious influence that can come to man.

What earthly good can give joy like this? Death robs us of every crown of joy but this! Gold, fame, honor, and earthly success are all silenced in its presence! Only Jesus can give triumph over death because He holds its keys. Joy in Jesus Christ is unwithered by death's touch.

Come, let us anew our journey pursue,
With vigor arise,
And press to our permanent place in the skies:

Of heavenly birth, though wand'ring on earth,
This is not the place,
But strangers and pilgrims ourselves we con-
fess.

At Jesus' call we gave up our all;
And still we forego,
For Jesus' sake, our enjoyments below:
No longing we find for the country behind;
But onward we move,
And still we are seeking a country above—
Charles Wesley.